Pack

"Only from deep pain could come ~~these~~ ... ~~tools~~ ... ~~tools~~ for surviving the darkness."

—Elizabeth Sherrill, bestselling author
Roving Editor, *Guideposts* magazine

"*When He Leaves* will give uplifting and inspirational challenges to the women who have endured overwhelming loss from a broken marriage. It will jump-start them on the road to becoming well again...offering encouragement that will be like fresh water to a thirsty soul."

—Barbara Johnson, bestselling author

"Kari West and Noelle Quinn invite you to share in their personal healing process. Carefully avoiding old-hat fix-it advice, they demonstrate that life not only will go forward, it can be done with a richer and deeper awareness of God's tender guidance and care."

—Les Carter, PhD, counselor, Minirth Clinic
author of *Grace and Divorce*

"An empowering book for women experiencing the crucible of divorce...I believe this book will be a cherished how-to-survive manual for those who want to go from being a victim to one who triumphs."

—Nancie Carmichael, author, founder of Virtue Ministries

"This book is important for pastors and those working with the divorced...As portrayed and supported in this book, the proclamation of grace and forgiveness in divorce does not dilute Christian standards. It rather strengthens them."

—Dr. Paul E. Larsen
president, the Evangelical Covenant Church

"Kari West and Noelle Quinn recount their own journeys through 'divorce country' and offer what they have learned to help those struggling to accept, adjust, and create a new beginning. *When He Leaves* loudly proclaims that, with God's help, there is life beyond divorce!"

—Jim Smoke
author of *Growing Through Divorce*

"Powerful scab-scraping honesty, empathy, vulnerability...what encouragement and hope-giving is contained in these pages. I'm a woman living out the truth of this book...The emotions, thoughts, the soul of it are exactly where I have been—and am."

—Dr. Karen J. Hayter, former host and producer
of *COPE,* nationwide call-in television program

"Rooted in vivid, realistic experience, this book deserves to rise to the top of the lists for women in whatever stage of divorce."

—Dwight Small, author
professor emeritus, Westmont College

"Kari and Noelle...stood with their pain. Through acceptance and persistence, they found what every redeemed divorced woman discovers 'when he leaves'—God's grace is sufficient."

—Ingrid Trobisch, author
founder, Family Life Ministries, Quiet Waters Center

"As a professor of clinical psychology and a therapist, I greatly look forward to recommending this work to my students, clients, and all who suffer similarly—as well as to professionals in helping positions."

—Gary H. Strauss, EdD, associate professor,
Rosemead School of Psychology, Biola University

When He Leaves

Kari West &
Noelle Quinn

HARVEST HOUSE PUBLISHERS

EUGENE, OREGON

Cover by Koechel Peterson & Associates, Inc., Minneapolis, Minnesota

WHEN HE LEAVES
Copyright © 1998 by Kari West and Noelle Quinn
Published by Harvest House Publishers
Eugene, Oregon 97402
www.harvesthousepublishers.com

Library of Congress Cataloging-in-Publication Data
West, Kari.
   When he leaves/Kari West and Noelle Quinn.
      p. cm.
   Includes bibliographical references.
   ISBN-13: 978-0-7369-1586-1 (pbk.)
   ISBN-10: 0-7369-1586-9 (pbk.)
   1. Divorced women—Psychology. 2. Divorced women—Religious life. 3. Divorce—Psychological aspects. 4. Divorce—Religious aspects—Christianity. 5. Separation (Psychology) I. Quinn, Noelle. II. Title.
   HQ814.W48 2005
   306.89'3—dc22   2004022260

Printed in the United States of America

08 09 10 11 12 13 14 / VP-MS / 10 9 8 7 6 5 4

To women—

those who played a part in our lives,
the few whose selfless efforts made this book possible...
and the many who, reading these words,
know exactly why we wrote them.

Acknowledgments

We are indebted to all those who believed we could talk about divorce with redemption. Humiliation with dignity. Private pain with transparency and truth. We want to thank the following:

Mt. Hermon Christian Writers Conference, Mt. Hermon, California, for bringing us together. Harvest House Publishers for affirming our vision and bringing this book back into print. Debbie Alsdorf, women's ministry leader, whose discovery of this book shortly after its original release ignited a passionate advocacy for its life-giving message.

Arlene Somerville and Jeanette Thomason for reading the finished manuscript on midnight oil after working day jobs. Dwight Small, Steve Severs, and the Bay Area Writers Critique Group for their feedback. Patricia Cousins and the reference librarians at the Alameda County Library for collateral information. Ingrid Trobisch and Dr. Larry Vold for their inspiration.

Sharon Kinard, for interceding for our protection throughout the writing process. Ethel Herr and the Literature Ministry Prayer Fellowship, who faithfully prayed for our discernment. Our parents for loving us and raising us to love our husbands and families. Kari's husband, Richard, for his support, encouragement, and affirmation.

—*Kari and Noelle*

Contents

Foreword

⁓⟡⟡⟡⁓

I met Noelle and Kari nine years ago on the Colorado Springs campus of Focus on the Family. That organization had just released my book *An Affair of the Mind*. Noelle and Kari were looking for a publisher for the first edition of *When He Leaves*. Their marriages had ended because of their husbands' secret involvement with pornography and the acting out that accompanies that addiction. I was still married because, even though my husband had acted out as well, he was in recovery...and hope springs eternal. (For those of you not up on addiction vocabulary—"acting out" means they'd cheated on us big-time.) The three of us were going to talk with Dr. Dobson about how pornography affects marriages.

So, there we were—three first-time authors about to be interviewed on a program that most Christian authors would give their eyeteeth to be on. Because the audience is so huge, being on Dr. Dobson's program is roughly the equivalent of being on *Oprah*. As an author, it's to die for. And dying we were, but not because we had visions of huge royalty checks dancing in our heads. We were dying because we were about to open up our private shame and share it with the world. We were dying because it was still so hard for us to believe *our* lives had turned out *this* way.

After all, we were capable, attractive women who loved God and were faithful to regular Bible study, personal devotions, and private prayer. Devoted to hearth and home, we'd married Christian men and had repeatedly gone to the church for help with our troubled marriages. We'd been told to submit, be nicer, pray longer, and try harder—and we *had*. We knew some of the people listening would think we weren't godly enough, sexy enough, smart enough, or healthy enough—because, obviously, we would have caught on sooner if we hadn't been so messed up ourselves.

All this flooded before us as we knelt in the chapel to pray before the broadcast.

Then we dried our tears, squared our shoulders, and marched to the microphones, holding you in our hearts because we knew you were out there. But we had no idea how many of you there were. That broadcast opened the floodgates. In the years since, we've helped, talked to, and comforted multitudes of brokenhearted women, because about 50 percent of married Christian men and multitudes of pastors are secretly masturbating to porn. Porn addiction is harder to break than cocaine addiction, and porn addicts more likely to recidivate than any other type of addict. This $10-billion-a-year industry is killing our marriages.

Now divorced myself, I was overjoyed when I discovered that *When He Leaves* was going to be available again. This book is a giant hug for women who've had their lives shattered by their spouse's infidelity. As I read it, I laughed and then I cried and then I laughed some more.

Noelle and Kari "get it." They get how betrayal obliterates the spouse's sense of self. They get the feelings of powerlessness that overwhelm you when despite your best efforts, the prince you're kissing turns into a frog. But, most of all, they get the awesome joy that comes from sweeping up the broken pieces of your heart and pasting them together to create a new life that's a work of art.

Through pages that are more poetry than prose, Noelle and Kari open their warm, wise arms and pull broken women close, comforting them where they hurt and reminding them that no matter how dark the betrayal is, joy does come in the morning.

—*Laurie S. Hall*
author of An Affair of the Mind

A Personal Word
from the Authors

—⟨℧⟩—

Within every life story there is a love story—first love, rekindled love, or love lost. Like moths, we are drawn to love's flame here in this book. Flipping through scribbled journals, we will ourselves to come close to the pain. Not being consumed by it as we hold it in hand is the miracle of what we've come to know.

No silence is loud enough to drown the echoes of our experience; that is why we write. But our words shed only a flicker of light on a much larger picture. This is a composite of two separate stories. There is much more we do not say than we do say. We juggle the enormity of what we feel needs to be said with saying nothing at all. We cannot give you the definitive account. We give you our personal reflections on truth that surfaced as we searched for our voice and our footing in this most earthly of human errors, divorce.

Our joint desire is not to air dirty laundry, dump our garbage in your backyard, or get even with our ex-spouses, both brilliant men whom we wish well. Their names and those of our families and others have been changed. We write not to be provocative or sensational, and we intend no malice. We are not bitter— although we are frustrated by the trend of wives dumped in midlife and children abandoned, and by the response of the church to a crisis that occurs no less frequently within evangelicalism than outside it.

Although we fought to keep our marriages intact until the very end, we have since gone on with our lives. In the course of that, we hear the screams of women. This is our bottom line. For the many who journey this way, for the many who will travel the same path, as well as for those who want to understand, we write. But this is not an appeal to the intelligence and emotions of women only. We hope every church leader and worker—especially those involved in men's and women's ministries—will read this account and wrestle through these issues with us for the sake of other families.

Between the two of us we have four daughters, quite an investment in femininity. Innocent and accomplished, they mean more to us than words can say. They may never read our stories, but our daily prayer is that they find healing and one day be cherished by mates who are faithful and true. Our desire is that each enjoy a healthy, ongoing relationship with her father.

To frightened souls looking for courage to take steps back into life, love, and laughter, opening the pages of this book may mean that you, too, will touch your pain. We understand. Read it at random, a quote now and then, or a chapter out of order. Absorb what you can, when you can. Then write to us.

We have been through something profound. This book is our labor of love.

You're Not Alone

—⟨∘⟩—

You are not alone. You belong to a sacred sisterhood, the wounded, the rejected, the betrayed. You are seeing truth, and in the horror of its light are shaken, battered, and bruised. But you do not give up. You get onto bloodied knees and start to crawl forward again. Like a drowning woman, you reach out for a life-saver, anything floating.

You are not thinking about recovery or rebuilding or happiness right now. You just want to survive. For your kids. For your parents. For some unexplained something deep down inside that makes you hang on even when you'd rather slide into the cold waters, be submerged, and disappear.

It would be better to die, you sometimes tell yourself. But something keeps you coming up for air, more light, more truth. You pray for courage to stand what you see. A week, a month, a year seems too long to count. You hope for the strength to get through the next moment, the next hour, the next day.

We have come through these same waters. Deep waters. We know the feelings, the fears, the rage, the terror. Let us take your hand, put an arm around your shoulder, swim beside you for a while. We cannot bring you to safety. Only you can find the life ring that will finally pull you up and out of the cold and the dark. But we can whisper, *Hang on! Hold out!*

By the goodness of God our Father, the same God you may have cursed a time or two, you will find the way. In the comfort of the Holy Spirit, who is closer than your breath, you will know increasing degrees of peace, sanity, and at last—at long last—joy. In the fellowship of the Son, Jesus Christ, you are loved and accepted exactly as you are, desired, and enfolded in arms tender and strong.

You are graceful, beautiful, and sensual. You are to be treasured and cherished. Proverbs 4:18 says you are like the light of dawn, growing brighter and brighter until full daylight. We wait with you and watch. You'll see.

—Kari and Noelle

Chapter One

We Know You

I am afraid;
My courage is gone...
I lift my hands to you in prayer.
As a dry land needs rain, I thirst for you.
Lord, answer me quickly,
Because I am getting weak.

—PSALM 143:4,6-7 NCV

We would know you anywhere. We see you everywhere: crossing a street, sitting behind stacks of paperwork at the next desk in the office, waiting in line at the grocery checkout, serving as greeter at the church door on Sunday morning. We see you at the gym, the PTA, the Bible-study potluck, the county fair, and the doctor's office. Sometimes we ask, "How are you?" and you always answer, "Fine!" or "Great!" But we know the truth.

We notice what many others do not: the limp smile disguising your fear, the lump in your throat right above your necklace, the pain deep in your eyes that no makeup can cover. Sometimes, if we venture closer, we feel the ground quivering beneath your feet. We sense the path you're on and sigh about what lies before you.

We've felt the jabbing pain you feel when you hear the love song you shared with him, when you hear two lovers say, "I love you." You think no one will whisper those words in your ear again.

And that family picture in the church directory? "Okay, now," the photographer said, "everybody think love." No one knew you were thinking daisies...*He loves me not.*

We know about the photo albums in your cupboard and the way you avoid that corner of your house. We know about that treasured recipe book you tossed out in fury, the one full of favorite requests you cooked for him through years of mealtimes. You have his love letters tied with ribbon in your bedroom closet. Your engagement ring and wedding band lie in the bottom of your dresser drawer, and you wonder what to do with them. Your eyes fill with tears at odd moments during your working day, and you hope no one notices.

At night, you've tried to put odd shapes and sizes of ragged suspicions together. You tried confronting him, but he always talked you out of it. *Love believes the best*—doesn't the Bible say that? *Love never gives up?*

But his working late became more and more frequent. Sometimes he left for work early or refused to get out of bed until you and the children left for the day. He'd crawl in late, and he didn't want to see anyone the next morning. He fussed about the noise the children made. And how dare you inquire about where he was—*working for you, of course; earning a living, of course.* Or sometimes he just said, "Give me space. Get off my case. You have nothing to worry about."

Once he told you his office phone was out of order and you'd have to leave a message if you needed to get hold of him. You never suspected he wasn't there at all. Another time, he left a party early to go back to work, just after your friend and neighbor excused herself to go home. You never thought a dishonorable thought about them.

When you said, "Let's make love tonight," he'd say, "I'm tired," or "I don't feel good." He obliged when you initiated, but his responses became less passionate. When you asked, "What's wrong?" he shrugged it off: "Oh, lots of men my age are impotent," or "I'm fine. I just don't feel like it tonight." You would lie in the darkness and pray he'd touch you back. But his touch became more and more infrequent even during the day. Your insecurities mounted, distancing him even more.

> *Love in action is a harsh and dreadful thing, compared with love in dreams.*
> —Fyodor Mikhailovich Dostoyevsky

When you finally found the nerve to ask the right questions of yourself and of him, he accused you: "You just don't get it." "You're too sensitive." "You're too black-and-white."

During a fight, he may have snarled, "You're crazy," or "What man would ever want you?" When you pleaded for romance and intimacy, he may have quipped, "Our marriage is fine. We'll do the best we can with what we have. It'll get better." And you believed him—until the roof started caving in on top of you.

Maybe a friend risked saying, "Do you think he's having an affair?"

You probably answered, "No. Not him. He'd never do that. We're a Christian family. We pray together, attend church." Maybe he is the one who raised his hands in praise, led the worship, helped with the young people's program. Perhaps he's the choir director, the youth leader, the elder, the deacon, the Bible-study leader—maybe even the pastor.

Another friend ventured, "Are you meeting his sexual needs?" Only you know the doubts you've agonized over, the magazine articles you've pored over, the questions you've put to your doctor, feeling desperate and determined.

Now, he is gone.

You are devastated by the images of what you did not know, did not recognize, could not admit. The accumulated pieces start to fall into place. Each unrelated message bouncing through your brain is beginning to make sense.

The great enemy of truth is very often not the lie—deliberate, contrived and dishonest—but the myth—persistent, persuasive and unrealistic.
—John F. Kennedy

We feel your searing humiliation and staggering pain. We hear your rage at yourself, at him, and at God. You ask, "How could this happen to me?" You wonder, *Does anybody care?*

We do. We are just like you.

We know the pathway you've been on, every stone you've stumbled over, the muddy ruts, the crevices leading off the edge.

We understand how you've thought so many times, *Something is wrong with this picture.* You kept telling yourself, *I cannot dwell on this.* You went on, distracted by the many duties and responsibilities before you. And that is just what he wanted.

Even as the confusion and hurt accumulated, you kept making meals, cleaning house, and caring for the children of a man who had long since left you in his heart and mind. So many people were counting on you: children, parents, friends, the church. Months passed. Years. Then one day the pot overflowed, the lies reached their zenith, the deceit could no longer be hidden.

You inhaled deception and exhaled horror. Now you wonder how you'll ever get yourself to your OB/GYN and ask for a set of STD and HIV tests in the wake of what you now know. How will you explain the humiliation or the way he indirectly threatened your life? You tell a counselor, "I can't be divorced. I can't be a single mom. I can't do *this*. This isn't how I planned my life."

You wonder how to tell your children. You promised they would never live in a "broken family," that you and their daddy would never get a divorce. How do you comfort them now or quell their fears when you have so many of your own?

We know. We, too, have stretched across an empty bed and howled into the black arms of the night. We are here to talk about those sacred, private spaces and the healing on its way to you.

> *Don't put your life on hold because somebody else changed the rules.*
>
> —KARI WEST

Did You Leave First?

Many of you may be reading these words and wondering if this book is for you. You're feeling guilty because you are the one who left, the one who filed for divorce. Perhaps he refused to file because he wanted to say you divorced him. Perhaps he believed his indiscretions, porn "hobby," or cases of microbrew were common fare for men—and therefore acceptable.

Just because you opted out doesn't mean you wanted the divorce. Experts say a primary reason women leave is because a husband has left long before in his mind, while he expected her to pray and stay. We want you to know this book is for those of you who also left him. Our hope is for healing and that you also may live, love, and laugh again.

Chapter Two
Kari's Snapshots

—☙☙—

I am seven years old. My mother lifts the lid on the cedar trunk at the foot of her bed, takes out a red fox boa, and drapes it around my shoulders. I squeal with delight, feeling glamorous and beautiful. I twirl like a top, my mind dancing in a world of Prince Charming kisses and his forever love.

—☙☙—

Mother sings a hymn to me: "I would be *true*, for there are those who trust me. I would be *pure*, for there are those who care. I would be *strong*, for there is much to suffer. I would be *brave*, for there is much to dare."[1]

Memory is a diary that we carry around with us.
—OSCAR WILDE

"Start praying for your future husband," the Sunday school teacher tells our ninth-grade girls' class. "Don't look for the right person; be the right person."

—◦◦◦—

At 18, I perch alone on a twin bed in sparse surroundings. Home is a rented room on the eleventh floor of a boardinghouse 2000 miles from my parents. I work days to pay for room, board, and night-school tuition. Listening to the grinding growl of buses on the street below, I'm content and happy, reading a love letter. Ed is stationed back East in the military. I met him at my home church last Christmas. Snow fell as he kissed me goodbye.

> *Love has various lodgings; the same word does not always signify the same thing.*
>
> —VOLTAIRE

I'm 22, in a bouffant wedding dress, walking down an aisle in shimmering candlelight. Ed promises, "Until death do us part." The minister prays, "May the Holy Spirit lead you into all truth." I smile and treasure Ed's words. Years later it is the minister's words I'll remember.

—◦◦◦—

Through the years, my job supports us while Ed completes his undergraduate and graduate degrees. I dream of being a stay-at-home mom, but it's not to be.

—◦◦◦—

Thirteen years later, I overhear a young woman at work tell another, "I want my marriage to be just like Ed and Kari's." Hopping into the elevator, I'm proud and happy. We have a two-story house with a water view and a darling three-year-old daughter, Melanie.

─◌◌◌─

Ed buys himself a flashy sports car. When Melanie and I visit my parents for a week in the Midwest, he purchases a motorcycle. Home again, I voice concern about little Melanie going for a ride with him. He accuses me of not trusting him, straps her to his belt, and guns the bike down the street. I think, *Wherever Ed is heading, I'm in his way.*

> *Mockery is the weapon that evil uses powerfully to strip its victim of a sense of self and life.*
> —DR. DAN ALLENDER

I injure my back. Ed complains when I ask his help making our bed, so I do it alone, crawling around its edges on my knees. Later, one Sunday afternoon, I walk into the family room. He is stretched out in his favorite chair. A porn video flickers on the TV screen.

"What are you doing?" I ask. "Our four-year-old is upstairs— what if she walks in here?"

"You're always starting fights," Ed says.

─◌◌◌─

Melanie's first-grade teacher recommends testing for behavioral and school problems. After Melanie is diagnosed with hyperactivity and a learning disability, I research the Feingold diet in my "spare" time. I'm hesitant about subjecting her to drug therapy and decide instead to cook meals free of artificial flavorings, colors, preservatives. It takes hours to check packaging labels at the market, to bake cakes so Melanie can bring a piece to eat at another child's birthday party, to attend parents' support-group meetings, and to tutor her after dinner. Ed doesn't believe the diagnosis and says we can't afford for me to quit work. *Doesn't anybody understand that I'm not sure how much more I can handle?*

—◌◌◌—

Melanie is taping her daddy's latest note to the railing of her canopy bed. Ed places one on her pillow each time he leaves on a business trip, a so-called group-counseling retreat, or weekend getaway. He says he's fighting memories of his mother's aban-donment and his parents' divorce. I try to understand and give him the space and time he needs to heal. I read every book in the library and Christian bookstore on midlife crisis and childhood trauma. But the answers don't connect with my questions. I think about all the notes above Melanie's bed. They bother me. But there is no one to ask about it. Someone did tell me Ed has a spiritual problem. It turns out to be close to the truth, but knowing it doesn't change things.

—◌◌◌—

When I can fit it in, I exercise twice a week before work. At the gym, I find a note tucked beneath my car's wiper blades: "Your husband is fooling around in your own backyard." Ed claims some-body at work is just playing political games. He plans to take it to the sheriff's office to have the handwriting checked. Grabbing the note, he says, "But I know you—you'll make a big deal out of this."

—⟨᪒⟩—

Warm water winds its way through the strands of my hair, bouncing off my shoulders, trickling down my back, spilling onto the tiles. I turn my face into the spray, praying for truth. My daughter can't hear me heaving with sobs when I'm here. Soap is a good excuse for puffy, red eyes. I come here more often now—whenever Ed's excuses and accusations pummel my mind like bricks.

> *It is only with the heart that one can see rightly; what is essential is invisible to the eye.*
> —ANTOINE DE SAINT-EXUPÉRY

The minister who counsels us keeps telling me I'm the stronger one and Ed is going through a midlife crisis. So for Melanie and me, I recommit myself to my man and my marriage once again. But now I'm pleading for truth.

—⟨᪒⟩—

I round the hill known as age 40 and feel less sure of my life. Ed and I are back together after a seven-month separation so he could "find himself." I work extra hours to provide a down payment for a weekend cabin in the mountains to give us a second chance, a fresh start, a new dream. Driving up to the cabin one weekend, he asks me to adjust the mirror on the passenger side. I tug and pull and then sigh, "It won't budge."

"Hurry, Mommy, I'm cold," Melanie says.

"You're so stupid!" Ed yells. "Can't you do anything right?"

"Yeah, Mom, can't you do anything right?" Melanie wraps her arms around her daddy's neck and snuggles in, glaring at me. *What did I do wrong?* I wonder.

—⟨⟩⟨⟩—

Ed's away again for the weekend. It's dark by the time I slide onto the organ bench in the living room, caressing the keys with my fingers. Through my tears, I can barely see the notes and words of "Because He Lives." Something is wrong, but I can't sort out my scattered thoughts. *How do I face tomorrow?*

A faintly penciled note Melanie left on the kitchen counter haunts me: "Dear Mom and Dad, I'm getting tired of you guys fighting and I always have to go to my room. I feel like I'm not part of this family. This house is always full of cries and hurt hearts."

I hold her up to God as I play the next verse, willing myself to believe my child can face whatever lies ahead because Jesus lives. How often have I imagined reaching for the doorknob? But I can't yank Melanie out of the only life she knows. Just because I'm hurting, I can't hurt her. My hands tremble as I play the last verse, longing for the day when my battle with life's pain will be over.

> *Next time I will forget about love and fall into chocolate.*
> —KARI WEST

Ed refuses to attend church now—or fix the washing machine. He never holds my hand anymore or wants sex. He says if it's so important I should get my calendar out and schedule it, so he can service me. I cry. He calls me "too sensitive," "crazy." I retreat emotionally.

⎯ↁↂ⎯

Ed works later and rises earlier, saying, if I inquire, that he's not accountable to me.

"But I'm your wife," I say. His dark eyes scare me.

⎯ↁↂ⎯

"Look at yourself! You're a nervous wreck," says my friend Regina. "I've never seen you like this. I know you don't believe in divorce, but are you honoring God with your marriage?"

⎯ↁↂ⎯

One weekend, Melanie, now 12, blurts out, "You don't even know where your own husband is."

I'm suspended in disbelief.

> *When I looked for good, evil came to me;*
> *And when I waited for light, then came darkness.*
> *My heart is in turmoil and cannot rest.*
> —JOB 30:26-27

"Ed, we need to talk," I get the courage to say again. "Something is wrong between us."

He slams his body against the back of his recliner as he flings the TV remote across the room. "And just what do you suggest this time?" he counters.

"Anything! Counseling again? Another separation? I don't know! Divorce?" I say in desperation, trying to shake up his usual mode of shutting me out.

"That's it! Divorce!" Ed cuts me off mid-sentence as if he's in a hurry. As if he's been waiting for me to say that word.

———

Fourteen days before Christmas, I sort the mail, a stack of season's greetings in one hand, a divorce summons in the other. That moment slashes 22 years of family holiday traditions and memories. I think back to cozy evenings before the fire, listening to carols and reminiscing over photos of a growing daughter sitting on Santa's knee.

Then I remember yesterday. Melanie screamed at me, "I don't want to be anything like you. I don't want to talk like you, dress like you, act like you, or look like you, because Daddy left you!"

I always trusted in a God who could turn evil into good. I wonder how he'll do it this time.

———

I believe God will reward my faithfulness with a miracle before the divorce is final. I kneel beside the bed and pray, *Lord, please save this marriage. I don't know what else to do.*

He whispers, "Let go and I will bless you." But I think I'm hearing things. *Letting go isn't what I want. I love Ed. I love being married. There are no grounds for this divorce.*

There is a time for departure even when there is no certain place to go.
—Tennessee Williams

"I've never been happier," Ed tells me, carrying the final box to his car. He says we should have divorced a long time ago.

"What?" I ask. "You can't mean that!"

Ed stammers. "I mean...earlier, so we didn't have to hurt Melanie," he says with a cocky toss of the head.

"Is there another woman?"

"No. But you have your desertion. And by the time the divorce is final, you'll have your infidelity," he says. "I like bleached blonds now with lots of makeup and long painted nails." He gets in the car and drives off.

I twirl strands of dark brown hair between my fingers, then stare at my short fingernails. *All those years I worked for us?* In a place beyond tears, I sob.

—❦—

"I'm glad you found out about the neighbor," says an acquaintance I haven't seen in ten years. She stands ahead of me in line at the bank the day after Ed and I finalize the paperwork and divide our assets.

"What neighbor?" I ask.

My friend shakes her head, then hurries toward the next available teller's window.

Oh, that I had wings like a dove! I would fly away and be at rest...I would hasten my escape from the windy storm and tempest.
—Psalm 55:6,8

Moving the car out of the garage one morning, my eye targets a stack of *Playboy* magazines under some junk Ed left behind. I also find a book about how to tell when people are lying. I wonder, *What else don't I know?*

—⟨⟩—

Melanie dials Ed's residence before school. A woman answers. Melanie dials again, convinced she has the wrong number. The female voice answers again.

"Just the cleaning lady," her dad later explains when she reaches him at the office.

I drive Melanie to school. "Mom, cleaning ladies don't answer telephones," she says.

I need to deal with this, but my job for the day is already assigned. Before getting on the freeway, I race back to the house and call Ed. "Even Melanie knows what you're up to," I say.

"You made sure of that, didn't you?" he says.

No, Ed, I didn't know until now, I say to myself as I place the receiver in its cradle. *I've always believed you—until now.*

—⟨⟩—

I move into the darkest tunnel of my life. I can't concentrate on my job. At night I toss and turn with dark, angry thoughts. It seems as if every day I learn something new about Ed: his secret post-office box, the names of "friends" he traveled with, that he'd given "her" a necklace identical to one he'd given me, that "group counseling" and "bowling" were two of many cover-ups. I flip through my Bible searching for answers, scribbling each promise I find in its margins and in a journal. With trembling hands I write angry letters to God, full of fear and disappointment. Somehow I must will myself to believe he still has plans for me. *Lord*, I pray, *give me courage for each day.*

_﹏ঌৎ﹏_

I sit across from Ed at a restaurant, signing our last joint tax return. He looks straight at me and says, "After what I did to you, you'll never trust anyone again."

My scalp lifts. I shiver before glancing past him, over his shoulder to the view outside. An ocean breeze tugs the tucked sails on the boats nestled at the harbor. A seagull soars above steel-gray water.

I reach for the pen and know I've chosen the only path, the way out, the way beyond.

> *The world is round and the place which may seem like the end may also be the beginning.*
> —Ivy Baker Priest

Moving on and into my own house is scary. My car breaks down. The sink leaks. The stove thermostat malfunctions. Melanie walks blocks to catch the city bus to and from school. Behavior problems escalate as her grades plummet.

I tiptoe into her bedroom. Gifts from Ed fill shelves—TV, stereo system, bowling ball, stuffed animals, leather jackets, $50 perfume, a dozen roses. Standing above Melanie's sleeping form, I whisper, "Protect her, Lord. Help me release her to you."

_﹏ঌৎ﹏_

One weekend, when Ed picks up Melanie, he tells me he isn't sure he has ever told anybody the truth; the worst lies are the ones he tells himself.

"And I loved you," I reply.

"I know," he says. "I wish you didn't. It would make it easier."

Wedged between compassion, numbness, and rage, I decide I am finally through reasoning with Ed. I don't want to hear another lie. I am tired of obsessing about who he is with, where he is, and what they are doing. I tell his dad on the phone, "I hope Ed dies of AIDS." Then I ask God to forgive me and help me determine to forgive Ed—not just for what he did but for what might be ahead. *Lord, I'm trusting you for my health, Melanie, my job, car, and the unknown future,* I pray.

Me, a single-again working mom, with time for a future? Impossible. My most blissful dream is of falling asleep and never waking up.

—⟨⟩—

Today, more than 15 years later, I don't want to remember the pain of that nightmare before Christmas—or the horror after. But I force myself to think about Ed's icy glares, his fists hitting the kitchen counter, the way he blamed me for ruining his life, how I cringed whenever his car pulled into the garage.

Ed seemed unendingly brash and insensitive. "To celebrate our amicable divorce," he said once, "I'll take you to dinner."

Celebrate? I thought. *You've left family, you're sleeping with someone else, and the ink isn't even dry on our settlement agreement.*

But I chuckle now. My future was God's surprise. I found a job closer to home, got another car, and happily gained back the weight I'd lost. I fell in love again. Richard still says I'm his best friend.

And Melanie? A while back she asked, "Mom, can I wear one of your necklaces tonight?"

I smiled, remembering the days when she didn't want to talk, dress, act, or look like me.

As I condense my experiences into these sentences, I realize I am writing for all of us—you, the reader; my daughter; and myself. This book gives Melanie no information she does not already have. Through watching me she has gained understanding of God's refining process and the person I am becoming. You see, the failure of my marriage to Ed was not a finish, but a fresh start. I found out when you can't go back, you go forward. I bought new photo albums, and I am just beginning to fill them. Now that's cause for celebration!

God is here this moment in the darkroom of your life. Let him develop the negatives into a positive image of his character to make you more like Jesus and to give you a future and a hope.

—KARI WEST

Chapter Three

Noelle's Snapshots

I will go before you
And make the crooked places straight...
I will give you the treasures of darkness
And hidden riches of secret places.

—Isaiah 45:2,3

⁂

I am walking down the sidewalk in the frilly blue-and-white ballet dress my mother sewed, pink slippers tucked under my arm. The studio is at the end of the block. At five years old, I feel independent and proud of myself. I am learning just how wonderful I am. When I grow up, I am going to dance stories on a beautiful stage.

⁂

My first day of kindergarten I see something I'd only dreamed of: a dollhouse filled with accessories. I kneel down and start to play with it, putting baby in the cradle, moving mother to the kitchen, seating father in the armchair. I imagine my someday-self in my someday-home. But I feel intimidated when another child comes along and moves things around. *Why is she taking it away from me?* I turn away.

> The LORD *is close to the brokenhearted and saves those who are crushed in spirit.*
> —PSALM 34:18 NIV

It's dark, but the bonfire is glowing on the last night of junior-high church camp. Our speaker, a missionary to the Philippines, asks us to throw a piece of wood in the fire and make our commitment to God. I sense his call to be a missionary. As I throw my piece of wood into the flames, I silently say *yes* to God and mean it with all my heart.

—⟲⟳—

Cowbells clink in the distance. I can't believe I'm in Switzerland! There'll be porridge and hot milk before we start our day working in the chalet or studying. I spend two years working overseas, also at a mental-care facility in England, a bed and breakfast in Austria, and a peanut farm in Israel. I love to travel, but I long for a life companion with whom to serve God and this world.

—⟲⟳—

Four years later, I marry Dan under an oak tree. He carves our initials in its bark. I carry a bouquet of tiny roses, standing barefoot in the grass. He sings Noel Paul Stookey's "Wedding Song" to me: "The union of your spirits here has caused Him to remain. For whenever two or more of you are gathered in His name, there is love."[1]

My dreams of going back overseas are coming true. We are heading there to evangelize. Dan is the man I prayed for, a man who loves God with a single heart.

We settle into our first home, two rooms in an old-world city. Dan moves in borrowed furniture. I decorate with remnants of fabric. We laugh about the tiny kitchen and plan our biweekly trip to the public bathhouse for showers.

Dan has friends here, many of them single women. I do my best to reach out, learn the language, and fit into the culture.

> *There are chapters in every life which are seldom read and certainly not aloud.*
> —CAROL SHIELDS

I wake up to the baby screaming. *Oh, no, not again.* I pull her cradle next to our bed. Why doesn't she just sleep? I am always tired; but worse, I am in a deep pit of despair. Fear grips me, while Dan turns over and goes back to sleep. I cuddle my perfect newborn girl as a strong and clear message comes from deep within my spirit: *Something is desperately wrong. It's a mistake with Dan.*

I am stunned, but chalk it up to postnatal depression. It must be lack of sleep. My husband provides for us now by working in the city, gone three to four days at a time. Taking care of our country home, I miss him, but comfort myself, knowing he is doing what he loves.

─◌◌─

We spend our first night in a new house. Early in the morning, nausea sweeps over me. I know this sensation. My period is late. At breakfast, I tell Dan, "I'm pregnant. I'm sure of it."

He is angry. "It's your fault. Why did you let this happen?"
I am stunned. By this pregnancy—but more by Dan's reaction.

—☙☙—

I tuck our three-year-old into bed and sit down to nurse our newborn. Dan is washing the dishes. Then he sits down with me. I look forward to the evenings together. He says he has to go back to the office. His job seems time-consuming and demanding, but when a pastor calls asking him to speak on relationships at a weekend retreat, he takes that on too. I question him, expressing frustration, but he brushes it off abruptly. He says I'm not letting him be a man. His comebacks are like a slap in the face, but I can't define the feeling. He showers, then gets in the car and drives away.

> *If suffering alone taught, all the world would be wise, since everyone suffers. To suffering must be added mourning, understanding, patience, love, openness and the willingness to remain vulnerable.*
> —ANNE MORROW LINDBERGH

Between his work and speaking engagements, Dan seems preoccupied and isn't home much. I read a slew of books. "If you and your spouse aren't growing together," they say, "you're growing apart." I tell him how I feel and ask, "Why don't you love me?"

"Your expectations are too big," he says.

We hear a sermon on marriage, and one line hits me: "If you aren't making love to your spouse at least once a week, you're too busy."

Why doesn't he hear this? I wonder.

―⟡⟡―

"I need you to plan a special occasion for our big anniver-sary," I say after the birth of our third child. "Somewhere nice." It sounds like a demand, but it's my way of saying, *I'm desperate for your affection.*

I juggle small children and a part-time job, and I need to know: Either he cares for me or he doesn't.

Dan plans a weekend anniversary trip—in connection with his business. He books a cheap flight and a cheaper hotel room. He isn't present emotionally. We spend the first night arguing. *Why is our marriage so difficult?* I keep asking myself.

―⟡⟡―

Dan blames our tensions on his job. We decide to move and start over. I support us now while he starts a small business.

"I hate those suits you wear," he says as I dress.

"I have to wear these to make a living for us," I tell him. His barbs snag my peace of mind. But he seems happy to spend the money I make on things he wants.

―⟡⟡―

During the day, Dan works from our home. Evenings, he finds a justification to see the "soccer match" at a pub downtown, meet "friends," or take a "photography safari." I wait up for him night after night, always crawling into our empty bed with an eerie ache.

"Give me space," he says when I ask why he avoids me. I blame it on his midlife crisis, his waning business, and my success.

"I'll be in the city all weekend working on a project," Dan informs me.

"Again? Why?" I counter. His two-day trips to a metropolitan area are increasing. "Can't you just do the research here?"

I feel uneasy about the reasons he gives me.

> *You did the best you could according to what you knew.*
> *And when you knew better, you did better.*
> —OPRAH WINFREY

"There's a late fee on your family account," the video clerk tells me. He reads the name of a movie returned late weeks before.

"I don't remember renting that," I say.

"No, I don't think you *would* rent that one," he answers with a wry smile. "But somebody on this account did."

Confused—and embarrassed—I pay the fee and leave quickly.

"Don't worry about the kids. Have fun," Dan says. He seems delighted each time I leave on a business trip. I'm proud of the way he jumps in and takes care of the house and girls. He seems proud of me and my job. I never worry about things when I go away.

But this time, I wake up in my hotel room the first night and feel a strong presence in the room. I don't often get on my knees, but this time I do. For several hours, I pour out my heart, compelled to pray for our marriage. I feel God is doing something good at last.

—☙❧—

Home again after an exciting ten-day trip, I can't wait to see my family and tell them about it. I believe things will be different with Dan and me. But he isn't at the airport to meet me. Half an hour later, he arrives, acting as if nothing is wrong. I'm in tears. He belittles me in front of our girls, blaming me for upsetting them.

Two days later, when we host a dinner party with friends to show pictures of my trip, his attention centers on a certain woman, a neighbor. He keeps pouring drinks for her and leaves "for the office" as soon as she makes her exit.

—☙❧—

Dan is out of town to visit his ailing father. I wake up sweating. I turn on the light and tell myself it was a nightmare. But my vivid dream of watching Dan and another woman in an erotic encounter haunts me. In the dream, I later ask him where he'd been and what he'd done. He sloughed off my suspicions and lied about it, not knowing I saw the whole thing.

In real life, when Dan returns home, I confront him with my dream and ask what he was doing while he was gone. He sloughs off my suspicions and shames me for an overactive imagination. I wonder, *Is he right?*

> *The private lie is in our face, violating the sanctity of our own nest—the place where we live, where we let our guard down…How easily we learn to turn down the volume on our own inner rumblings—the ones trying to alert us that something's going awry.*
>
> —DORY HOLLANDER

For our twentieth wedding anniversary we plan a weeklong trip to a romantic destination, though things are difficult between us. One week before we are to leave, Dan tells me we can't afford to go. I'm furious, but I bridle my emotions. I know I'll ruin what little relationship we have if I blow up.

We spend a weekend at a hotel close to home. Dan doesn't touch me or talk to me on the trip. I confront him with his lack of presence. He says, "I'm fine. I'm here. I'm enjoying myself. Why can't you let me be?"

I feel invisible in black lace.

―――

Working in the quiet of my home office, I sense a heavy blanket fall over me. *I know.* I know Dan is into pornography on trips to the city and in our home when I'm away.

"Isn't that true?" I ask when I call him at the office.

He sighs. "Yes," he says.

"You need to get counseling," I plead. "Deal with this. Pour out your gut to somebody. Get help."

He agrees.

―――

Several days later, I find by the bathroom sink a love letter posted from out of town. It's addressed to Dan, alluding to time in bed. When I ask him to explain, he looks both defiant and exposed.

"She didn't really mean this," he says. "You're taking it out of context."

For the first time, I know without a doubt he is lying. This is not an overactive imagination. Truth is there in black-and-white. He grabs the letter from my hand and leaves.

—ᏜᏜ—

After a flurry of phone calls that Dan always answers, he says finally, "There's something I have to tell you."

I brace myself.

He spills out details of an affair with another man's wife—not the person who had written the love letter.

"It didn't mean anything," he says. "She's in love with me now, but I don't love her. I'm cutting the whole thing off."

What is going on? How many are there? I wonder, unable to articulate my despair and his denial. My heart feels like a knife has been plunged into it. *I can't believe this is happening.*

> *Facing reality—knowing what we know, and knowing without a shadow of doubt that we know it—destroys our last shreds of optimism. There is no turning back. However painful, we're square with the truth; no use pretending we'll change or he'll change or somehow magically, everything will turn out right. In fact, everything is turning out right. We can't trade the rawness of reality for the more muted illusions we once held. But we can move forward with quiet confidence that we are holding tightly to the truth.*
>
> —ELLEN SUE STERN

"I'm not going to be depressed anymore," Dan tells me. "I'm leaving."

"Why?" I plead. "We can work this out. I love you. I want to stay married. For us. For the children. I can forgive you. I can change if you want me to. I can meet your needs if I just know what they are: kinky sex, anything."

"No. I've always needed something you're not."

"There's *another* woman?"

"No," he says.

"A man?" I manage a laugh.

"I just have to leave."

I beg him to stay just one more week—until our daughter's holiday performance. He agrees.

———⌒⌒———

"How do I look?" Dan says, a couple days later, giving his body a cool-guy shimmy.

"Whoa," I say. "You look great. Those neat boots! My favorite jeans. You know I love it when you dress like that."

Before he leaves, Dan wants to know if I'll be busy all day. "Oh, by the way," he adds, "my work phone is out of order." The next day is the same: cool clothes, phone out of order, "Will you be busy?" And the next. Finally I demand, "What's going on?" Dan names a certain woman, a neighbor: The Neighbor. "I've been in love with her for five years," he says through phony tears, adding a worn cliché: "She's my soul mate."

———⌒⌒———

Weeks later, Dan and I talk about how to tell our oldest child about our breakup. She is spending a semester abroad. I look straight into his eyes and blurt out words that erupt from my lips, "And I know about all your prostitutes and old girlfriends." *I can't believe I said that. I did not know any such thing; where did that come from?*

Dan glares at me. "Have you been talking to my counselor?"

"No," I say, still shocked by what I had said.

Numbness envelops me as Dan admits infidelity starting with our first year of marriage. "I had to do it," he says, adding, "I'm still a Christian." He leaves. I stay at my bedside for hours, stunned, immobile.

> *The best thing about the future is that it comes only one day at a time.*
>
> —Abraham Lincoln

A year before Dan left, I had christened the new year "A Year of Light." I wrote my prayer requests, including skylights for our home, in my journal. Little did I realize then how my prayer for light would be answered. Not in the way I expected! Exposure brought nauseating waves of pain and rage. My childhood dream to dance stories on a beautiful stage burst like a bubble. And that dollhouse? Someone else did come and move things around despite the fact that I was there first.

I crawled, trudged, and climbed through that year. I determined to feel the deep rage deeply, then leave it behind. Out of sheer will to survive, I forgave—in increments. I learned to look deeper and harder and to own the truth, no matter how painful. Today I know truth is worth clinging to, because it set me free.

One morning an acquaintance told me she was moving across the street from me. I'd seen her eyes swollen recently, the way mine looked last year. I said, "Look, if you're going through what I've just been through, I'm so sorry."

She said, "Well, how are you doing?"

"Oh, so much better," I told her.

She sighed with relief and said, "That's what I need to hear."

When I am here for others going the same direction, my own healing flows—a window through which I recognize that good comes knotted with bad and that joy is tangled up with pain. Accepting that has made me stronger and happier. The negatives continue to develop. Instead of dancing stories on stage, I'm using paper and pen.

> *Everything in your life is on time. Even this. Don't hurry the future. Live the present. Even embrace your pain. God will heal the past as you move forward one baby step at a time.*
>
> —NOELLE QUINN

Pornography Hurts

Forty million American adults visit Internet porn sites regularly, making up nearly half the number of visitors worldwide (72 million). A Focus on the Family poll shows 47 percent of families admit pornography is a problem in their home, while 53 percent of Promise Keeper men said they had viewed porn in the last week.

Internet-porn Web sites, with $2.5 billion in annual revenue, number 4.2 million (12 percent of all Web sites), and they lure first-time visitors at the average age of 11. From then on, 12- to 17-year-olds are the largest consumers of Internet porn with 80 percent multiple hard-core exposure among 15- to 17-year-olds.

The international porn industry's annual revenue, $57 billion worldwide, is larger than all combined yearly revenues of all professional football, baseball, and basketball franchises, and U.S. annual porn revenue, $12 billion, exceeds the combined yearly revenues of ABC, CBS, and NBC:

- adult videos: $20 billion
- escort services: $11 billion

- cable/pay-per-view/Internet/CD-ROM: $6.5 billion
- sex clubs: $5 billion
- phone sex: $4.5 billion
- child pornography: $3 billion
- novelties/other: $2.5 billion[2]

Internet realities:

- Sex is the number-one topic searched on the Internet.
- Porn-site architects were among the first to perfect full-streaming video and audio and to persuade apprehensive consumers to divulge credit-card numbers on the Internet, developing e-commerce.
- 2.5 billion e-mails per day are pornographic.
- 25 percent of all search-engine requests are pornography-related.
- 98 percent of 81 pastors surveyed (74 male) were exposed to porn; 43 percent intentionally accessed a sexually explicit Web site.

TV-sex realities:

- 75 percent of prime-time television in 1999 to 2000 included sexual content, the percentage having nearly tripled in ten years.
- Playboy's largest cable channel, Playboy TV, is available in 24 million of the nation's 81 million homes that receive either satellite, cable, or digital television.
- Sexual content is featured once every four minutes on network TV, with 98 percent of all sexual content having no subsequent physical consequences, 85 percent of sexual behavior having no lasting emotional impact, and nearly 75 percent of participants in sexual activity unmarried.[3]

Chapter Four

I Have God and Me

*The way of the good person is like the light of dawn,
growing brighter and brighter until full daylight.
But the wicked walk around in the dark; they can't
even see what makes them stumble.*

—PROVERBS 4:18-19 NCV

Kari: An old sequoia tree sprawls beside the trail at Calaveras Big Trees State Park two hours from my home. It fell before the grove was discovered in 1852.

I noticed it on a hike one day and marveled at the tree's dimensions: 17 feet in diameter and 300 feet long. It was hollow, like a tunnel. *Hey, this would provide shelter on a windy day!* I thought. *And what a safe place to spend a stormy night.*

I stepped through the opening. Ribbons of sunlight fell across charred splotches on the inside walls. "Fire-scarred," park rangers describe it. *Had the tree survived a forest fire? Or had people stopped for shelter and built a fire to warm themselves through a dark, cold night?*

The dark and cold—that's what I remember most about the first months of my divorce. *Will I ever find light and warmth?* I wondered then. I was stumbling in the dark while Ed seemed to be getting on with what he wanted, full speed ahead.

I found shelter, but not as I expected. Not in powerful revelations from God, but in the promise of his presence. It wasn't by being rescued by him financially or by another man emotionally. A smooth road drenched in bright sunlight didn't suddenly appear. I found shelter in the very center of my life's tragedy, a marriage disintegrated from within like a tree weakened by rot, fallen in disgrace.

I wasn't the first to crawl into the dark hollow and build a fire there for warmth and light. I won't be the last. But it took getting past the trauma of being lost and losing myself. In a complex series of events never asked for or expected, I noticed my path growing brighter as I moved ahead, lit by glowing embers from that early fire.

> *The loss of love is a terrible thing. They lie who say that death is worse.*
>
> —Countee Cullen

This Isn't How I Planned My Life

The dissolution of marriage is not a single legal event. It's a multifaceted emotional process "more destabilizing and wrenching than any other emotional crisis, including death," claims psychotherapist Joan Rossman, in practice 20 years.[1]

"Divorce," says Helen Richards, a World War II concentration-camp survivor, "was worse than Dachau had ever been. In the camp, I was young. It was not a personal thing. There was everybody else. I wanted to survive. But during my divorce, I wanted to die."

Richards, being interviewed by Dr. James Dobson, went on to say, "We had been married 24 years. I was afraid. I hurt. There was no place to go to hide. Nobody could understand what I felt."[2]

For many Christians, divorce includes personal shame, guilt, and feelings of failing God and the church. Still, even within the evangelical community, divorce rates do not differ from society at large.[3] The question arises, To what degree does church teaching on the sacrament of marriage help heal and head off broken families?

Dr. Neil Clark Warren, psychologist, marriage counselor, and author of *The Triumphant Marriage*, says, "I've come to believe that 75 percent of all divorces involve marriages in which at least one partner is emotionally unhealthy." He adds, "Marriages can't cure individual emotional problems."[4]

Neither can the church. Or a healthy partner, no matter how much she would like to or tries. If the unhealthy individual is not willing to own the problem, confess it, or seek personal restoration, the marriage is headed for disaster.

Patterns in the *When He Leaves* scenario have been becoming obvious since we began this project and started connecting with other women going through the same thing. We even coined the term "The Neighbor" because most of us seem to have one. Although each divorce is slightly different, there are few surprises. We began to wonder, *Why do these guys, who believe they've met the love of their lives, think they are original? Is there a book for Christian men on how to cheat successfully for 20-plus years?* Not that we know of.

But as our book went to the editor, complete with its present title, another hit the bookstores: *Should You Leave?* by bestselling author and psychiatrist Peter Kramer. Kramer's educated diagnosis of the male-leaving phenomenon is uncanny in its insightful validation of our stories. Intending to spare men, their wives, and their children years of pain, he discusses a man's sad unwillingness to entertain the possibility that the problem might be within himself.

In a section on "the woman down the street," Kramer says, "I know this neighbor." Calling her "Carmen," he lays out the issue frankly for his male readers: "Though she is no Gypsy—actually she…has lived for years in the same suburban house…[she] likes action, complications, intrigue, attached men. Once your family turmoil is resolved and you are out in the cold, you will not last a month with her. When you say you need Carmen…you are saying that your hedonic capacity is turned way down low so that it takes enormous stimulation to move you at all. We know that older men need younger women not because the men still have it but because they don't."

The husband will attend counseling, Kramer says, "not because he expects the sessions to be of any use but out of a formal obligation to the wife." "Though you will never admit it," he writes again to his male readers, "you feel unworthy of your wife, and less capable…" His thesis reaches a crescendo when he asks, "And what are we to make of your readiness to withdraw from contact with your children, whom you say you adore? The truth is, you can no longer feel pleasure in any sphere."[5]

The larger picture eventually shows that these men lose. We only wonder why they are the last to realize it. Not out to incriminate them, we wish them recovery of self; they have suffered, too. We are here to say to women who must regroup, "Forge on."

Divorce Trends

Since 1999, the U.S. government has no longer been collecting comprehensive, detailed statistics on marriage and divorce. However we know the following:

- More than 1 million divorces have occurred annually in the U.S. since the late 1970s,[6] and today more people are part of second marriages than first marriages.[7]
- In 1993, the U.S. Census Bureau reported that divorce is on the rise among older women.[8] Author Gail Sheehy writes, "Divorce is occurring with greater frequency among people aged 40 to 54, from 1.5 million in 1970 to 6.1 million in 1991.[9]
- More than 1 million children are affected by divorce each year.[10]
- In 1998, 2.2 million couples married and 1.1 million couples divorced, showing a "crude" divorce rate of 50 percent.[11]
- In 1999, there was one divorce for every two marriages in the U.S. The Rutgers National Marriage Project notes that the overall chances that a marriage will end in either divorce or permanent separation are close to 50 percent.[12]

The longer you've been married, the more difficulty you may experience going through a divorce. But no matter how many years you were married, when he leaves and the shock begins to wear off, you face

- intense emotions, including grief, guilt, anger, hopelessness
- stress-related health problems
- disappointment with friends, family, church, and God
- upheaval of financial stability, social context, and family issues
- a deep sense of failure, humiliation, and rejection

How will you survive the emotional roller coaster, let alone rebuild your life? You will survive and move on because...

- When you feel, you heal. You are an integrated human being. Spiritual, mental, and emotional healing are interconnected with physical well-being.

- You are on a journey discovering what is real and what is not. As Jesus said in John 8:32, "You shall know the truth, and the truth shall make you free."

- You will learn a new skill we call "turnabout thinking." It will change all the "dis's" and "des's" in your life (disappointment, disillusionment, disarray, despair, desertion, despondency) into building blocks for a brand-new you.

Are You Going Crazy?

The specific losses of divorce and each woman's reaction to them are individual. Here are a few issues the two of us faced differently.

My Faith

Noelle: When a friend told me her divorce helped her grow because her faith in God went from 0 to 100 percent, I told her, "Well, my faith went from 100 percent to 0. Everything I've ever believed will have to be rebuilt from the ground up." Rebuilding was a painstaking and tenuous process.

> *Blessed are those whose dreams are shaped by their hopes and not by their hurts.*
> —ROBERT SCHULLER

Kari: My faith stayed intact and helped me through. In joint counseling before, during, and after our seven-month separation, I poured my heart out while Ed sat in stony silence. This was two years before the divorce. I can still see him, just home from one of the sessions, standing beside the freezer in the garage: "You and your faith," he accused. "You're always so Goody Two-shoes." With strength that was not mine, I stepped toward him. "Don't you ever— ever again attack my faith in God." I said. "It's all I *really* have."

Philip Yancey on Hope

Prisoner-of-war accounts indicate that some POWs may die for no apparent reason other than a loss of hope. Hope means simply the belief that something good lies ahead. It is not the same as optimism or wishful thinking, for these imply a denial of reality…Realistic hope permits a dying person to confront reality, but at the same time gives strength to go on living.[13]

—Philip Yancey

The Family Home

Noelle: I kept my home, working out an arrangement for payment with Dan, who respected my boundaries there. But living in the same small town not far from him and only a few streets from The Neighbor was painful. Friends asked, "How can you do it? Don't you want to move? Won't you have to in order to survive?"

My stubbornness came to the rescue. "This is my home," I countered. "This is my town, my place. I did nothing wrong. I can hold my head high. I'm staying." It was very hard for a long time. Finally, Dan's girlfriend moved and became someone else's neighbor.

> *Better a dry morsel with quietness, than a house full of feasting with strife.*
> —PROVERBS 17:1

Kari: Our family home had to be sold. Before the escrow closed, Ed moved out; but he came and went unannounced, whether I was home or at work, until I changed the locks.

"This is my home now," I told him. "We need ground rules we both understand. I'd appreciate it if you would not be in the house without me present, just as I'm not in your home. And please call before you come."

After I moved into a home of my own, my physical and emotional safety became top priority. I needed Melanie's cooperation to ensure that my personal boundaries and our joint privacy were not violated. She had to sit alone in the garage after school a few times until she promised not to let her dad inside when I wasn't there. When she threatened to go live with him because I had "only one bath and lousy green carpet," I endured her complaints.

Jim Smoke on New Beginnings

Divorce often keeps you living at the burial site of your marriage. The primary reasons are children, job, support systems, and family ties...If you have children, moving [to another area] is virtually impossible because the courts recognize the need for the other parent to be physically present in your children's lives. Moving with children usually demands the other parent's permission. We all need fresh starts and new beginnings after a crisis. It may mean that you can only move across town rather than across the country. [14]

—Jim Smoke

Sexual Trauma

Noelle: I was devastated by the revelation of my Christian husband's infidelities. I struggled with issues of femininity and sensuality. *Why hadn't he desired me? Wasn't I good enough? How could I have been so blind, accepting his explanations when I was sometimes suspicious? What were the needs he now claimed I wasn't meeting? Would any other man love and desire me?*

I was brokenhearted. But I met others going through the same thing who were coping with STDs and the fear of AIDS from their ex-husbands. My counselor explained sexual addictions and the pathological lying that accompanies them. She urged me not to believe his claims of abstinence; I needed to be tested. I hadn't believed him anyway, but just asking for those tests was the ultimate degradation. It took a long time to get up the nerve to go to the doctor.

The man I loved had taken advantage of my innocence, virginity, and submissive attitude. He, of all people, knew how much I prized my health and our sexual relationship. Who knew how many people I had been coupled with through his lifestyle? It took a long time for me to realize his lying extended beyond covering his tracks and the things he had claimed were true. I finally realized that in order to validate his dissipated masculinity, he had to believe the lies himself.

> *The orgasm has replaced the cross as the focus of longing and the image of fulfillment.*
> —Malcolm Muggeridge

Kari: Ed changed when I became a mother. He started accusing me of "not meeting his needs." But when I asked what they were, he didn't know. Over the years, I purchased slinky negligees and planned a vacation to Hawaii; but the first thing he hit on was the TV remote. I felt immobilized and depressed by his avoidance— exactly where he wanted me! A month after he filed for divorce, I requested an AIDS test because I was suspicious, though I had no substantial proof of infidelities. That night I wrote my first journal entry, based on 1 Peter 2:21-24: "Jesus, my example...uttered no threats...but kept entrusting himself to him who judges righteously." When I learned of Ed's affairs, I was both humiliated and furious.

Media coverage of the AIDS crisis shook my core and still does. I had felt "safe," since he was the only man I'd slept with.

Eventually I met The Neighbor. She apologized. I said I'd try to forgive her. Together, we matched the "business trips" with "the rendezvous" and pieced together Ed's excuses with reality. She had no idea she was one of his many "other women." At last I realized Ed had a big problem, and it wasn't me.

Dwight Small on the Internal Breach

Christian marriage rests upon more than an initial covenant; it rests upon the fidelity of each spouse to the other…"What God has joined together…" Adultery, upon which we tend to place such singular emphasis, represents an external [visible] breach…

An internal [invisible] breach in thought or attitude can also break the covenant. It is known only to the one who is secretly pulling away. But if left to continue, the process becomes irreversible in time, except for God's intervention. Covenant unity can be broken because one or both spouses walk away from its obligations or turn off mentally or emotionally…

Whenever a spouse is aware of being no longer committed to covenant goals or obligations to marital unity as total partnership or to a loving mutuality, then the covenant is beginning to come apart. Sexual infidelity then is symptom, not cause. Divorce then merely gives decent burial to the marriage that died—or was murdered![15]

—Dwight Small

Financial Stress

Noelle: Just prior to Dan's leaving, I lost my job and most of my friends when the company I worked for moved out of state. I started to freelance, but the decision to do that had been based on Dan's emotional and financial support. Now, traumatized and alone, I found it hard to produce the work. When I barely got my feet under me with a few projects, he said he couldn't make child-support payments as per our agreement. How perfectly timed. I realized it's never over—even post-divorce.

I envied divorced friends who were well set up, but I told Dan, "Fine. Default. I'll make it anyway." I traded my used car for a cheaper model with better mileage, borrowed on life insurance, and used my credit card for groceries. Friends told me, "Don't be too proud to receive." Family members found ways to offer help— a load of wood or gifts they knew the children needed.

I did something I'd never done before: prayed for money, lots of it. I worked and waited. At times God's silence was deafening. My work came through. Dan missed only one payment. That month I got an unexpected reimbursement from a company in just the amount I was short. Slowly I began to inch forward.

> *Better is a dinner of herbs where love is,*
> *Than a fatted calf with hatred.*
> —PROVERBS 15:17

Kari: I was self-employed, without the security of a salary or of health, disability, or vacation benefits. Being on call at three different firms meant I seldom knew before six o'clock each evening whether I had a job the next day. I drove more than 100 miles a day; gas and car repairs were a big expense. I managed to support my daughter on what I made, plus minimal child support.

I had no time or energy for games, such as when Ed handed me a year's worth of predated child-support checks and three months later canceled the account. I knew if I were tied up in the legal system I would miss time from work, lose income, and spend more money on attorney and account fees than I would ever collect from Ed. I determined to show him I didn't need him or his child-support checks, and I adjusted my standard of living accordingly. Through the advice of my attorney, my pastor, and my parents, and through my devotional reading, I kept hearing, *Let go and I will bless you.* That didn't mean God removed my financial needs, but he helped me meet them.

Individual Priorities

Noelle: We didn't think twice about keeping our dog, because he was almost like one of the children. But we did begin to economize, excluding luxuries like soda pop and red meat from the larder and making fewer trips to the store—any store. Clothing, dental checkups, and movies were out of the question for a long time.

> *Where your treasure is, there your heart will be also.*
> —MATTHEW 6:21

Kari: When a representative from Pets-In-Need drove off with our dog, I was devastated. But I couldn't afford to keep her and our cat, too. After I found out the rep was the widow of my favorite doctor, I took it as a positive sign that our dog was in good hands. Ed played off my guilt by telling Melanie how cruel I was to get rid of *her* dog. She didn't understand I had no choice. I felt awful.

Let's Face It!

According to Carol Ryff,[16] well-being is the presence of six life qualities:

* independence

- the ability to cope with complex demands
- feeling of growth as a person
- good relationships
- goals that give life meaning
- an acceptance of the self and the past

Divorce forces you to face yourself in light of these six life qualities. When you get on the other side, you realize waves of anxiety, anger, and regret inundate you from time to time; but if you think about it, your fears aren't much different from other people's in today's changing, unpredictable world. Others are scared, too—about losing their jobs, growing old, being alone. They have regrets about wasting their youth and not spending enough time with their children.

Divorce makes you face your vulnerability sooner, as would a chronic disease or a disability. In facing vulnerability, you become more reachable and transparent.

Perhaps you were taught vulnerability and transparency were not good. You were taught to keep your personal concerns to yourself. As one 1927 book put it, "It is women's duty to fill the home with sunshine and cheer…like a chirping bird." As you allow yourself to be transparent through crisis, you realize how appropriate, how very positive and healing, it is to be who you are.

The best remedy for a bruised heart is not, as some people seem to think, repose upon a manly bosom. Much more efficacious are honest work, physical activity, and the sudden acquisition of wealth.

—DOROTHY L. SAYERS

Kari: In my home, a one-of-a-kind vase is perched on a shelf. I bought a similar one for Noelle. They're fashioned from sections of 70-year-old juniper fence posts found in Montana. In the hands of artist John Noyes, the top part of each section has been sanded smooth, revealing fine swirling colors of rust and gold. A glass vial has been inserted to hold a sprig of wildflowers. The bottom half remains in its distressed form—rugged, gray, knotted, gnarled, pierced with a rusty nail or two.

From a living, breathing tree…to a felled log…to a weathered fence post…to a vase…the raw material found service and beauty. And in the creative hands of a loving God, so will you.

P.S.—You'll see.

I Have God and Me

Heart Work

I will turn my "dis's" and "des's" into building blocks for a new me.

In five or ten years this desertion might

- develop in me a new sense of poise.
- help me discover a new purpose.
- cause me to pursue a new passion for life itself.

I can imagine at least three gifts that may be hidden in my disappointment:

1.

2.

3.

Chapter 5

My Hope Is Increasing

By you I can run against a troop;
By my God I can leap over a wall.
As for God, His way is perfect;
The word of the LORD is proven;
He is a shield to all who trust in Him.

—2 SAMUEL 22:30-31

Noelle: I love the picture by artist Mary Engelbreit of the woman sitting in a rocker, patching up a torn and ragged heart. The view from her window shows a winding trail to the horizon. But her attention is focused on the important thing right in her lap.

In mending, my first instinct was to protect the hurt muscle from further injury. I couldn't rush emotional healing, just as a doctor can't hurry the healing of a broken bone. Instead, the doctor immobilizes it in a cast. Given time and protection, it will heal itself.

Sometimes I sat and rocked the reality of my divorce: wailing or whimpering. My tears cleansed and softened the wound. When I allowed myself to feel my feelings, not demanding too much too soon, I was doing something nice for myself.

What I remember most about those first months was the waiting—waiting for something good to happen and wondering if it ever would. But while rocking, I discovered simple tools to craft strong, even decorative, stitches in the heart: the beautifully colored threads of friendship. Sharp scissors to snip away frayed edges, snags, and dead ends. Needles in different sizes to accommodate the always-changing fabric of my life.

What really broke a heart was taking away its dream.
—PEARL BUCK

When the Dream Dies

Divorce is learning to live in serenity with your losses. Experts say that under normal circumstances a person's energy is distributed equally in four areas: spiritual, physical, mental, and emotional. During divorce, 85 percent of your energy goes to emotional coping. The remaining 15 percent goes to the other areas combined. That's why, running low on spiritual energy, you have trouble praying; low on mental energy, you have trouble concentrating; low on physical energy, you feel exhausted.

You go through the motions, the practical steps: the lawyer's meetings, the settlement agreement, the packing, the furniture-moving, the final decree. Then out of nowhere, when you think you are finally getting somewhere, you remember the little girl whose dreams were ripped off.

So be kind to yourself as you mend and patch. Your broken heart is drawing almost all your energy right now. Don't be embarrassed by scar tissue. In time, it leaves the skin stronger...and shows you've been through something you somehow wish you hadn't and yet are rather proud you have.

Kari: I shut the garage door and backed my car out of the driveway into the street. The sun dipped low on the horizon, drenching the house in a purple-pinkish glow. Yellow daffodils danced along the front walkway of our family home, the one I was leaving forever.

My eyes scanned the plastic bags and boxes awaiting charity pickup along the front porch. They bulged with odds and ends I no longer had room to store. At first I thought, *I'm seeing things.* One of the bag seams had torn. Taffeta and lace spilled out and flapped in the breeze. *This is the way a marriage ends*, I thought. *The skirt of my wedding dress is waving goodbye.*

> *A woman's tender heart bleeds when soaked with rejection.*
>
> —KARI WEST

Noelle: I forced my legs to carry me up the stairs to Dan's new apartment, though I didn't want to see him or his new place. The evening was cold, and snow lay in small drifts against the steps. I was lugging the last of his things from our home: a couple of screwdrivers, a box of assorted screws, and the wall plugs he'd asked for.

Dan stepped outside the door, and I caught a glimpse of a painting leaning against the wall inside, the one he'd proudly given me on one of our anniversaries. He invited me in to see the secondhand bed he'd just repainted and antiqued; but I declined, refusing to imagine who was going to sleep in it with him. I handed over the things.

This is the way a marriage ends, I thought. *And he gets the screws.*

Put Rage to Prayer, One Day at a Time

by Noelle Quinn

Dear Lord, dear Grace,

I call you Grace instead of God, for that is who you are. I need your grace today. Within me is a vicious anger. It is burning throughout my chest, even throughout my body. I cannot quench the raging flames, nor do I want to. This furious rage feels justified to me. Surely, it is only right to feel this way. Anger surges in waves of pain as I go about my day. I cannot contain this fire. Now, I drag myself before you exactly as I am. I believe you understand my desperate feelings. Do you? Your Word says I may come to you just as I am. Here I am, Lord.

Dear Grace,

I want things back they way they were. I want everything to be all right again. I am enraged by the wrong perpetrated against me. Stunned, like prey attacked by a snake in the grass, I am experiencing shock and unspeakable pain. How am I to endure, O Lord? How am I to get through this? My anger and hate feel powerful—the only tools I have to stand up instead of melt away. The only way forward, fueling my momentum toward the future. I cannot sense your presence right now, O Lord, but I thank you for listening anyway.

Dear Grace,

My rage is inspired by the person who wronged me, betrayed me, rejected me, then stomped on everything precious to me. I see only evil and lies. I want my rage to act as a holy power, causing him as much anguish as he caused me. I live with the repressed anger of my children and their confusion and pain. Why did this have to happen to us, Lord? What did we do to deserve this? Why must we pay the price for his sin and abomination? Still, my love for my children along with my desire to live with integrity cause me to ask for your mercy and grace. Please help me not to wrong my children in the wake of my rage or endanger the frightened little girl within myself.

Dear Grace,

My rage is caused by horrendous fear. Fear is the opposite of love, and the most powerful evil in the world. I've heard that hate is not the opposite of love, but very closely related to it. I hate because I loved so truly. I want to see some meaning in this crisis. I want to believe that something good can come of it. I want to know with all my heart that everything is exactly as it is supposed to be right now because all things come sifted through your great love for me. I don't feel like choosing to forgive. The other person doesn't deserve it. But with an act of defiance, I choose your will above my own will to simmer in this rage. I take the first step to will to forgive.

Dear Grace,

I can't forget the wrong done to me. I can't undo the damage. I can't change anyone's mind, and I see that even you won't change another person's heart if they choose not to change. So I ask for clarity and light to lead me on the way into a future I did not want. I receive that now in the name of Jesus. You say I am beautiful and lovable and beyond the value of diamonds. In faith, I let go of my rage as much as I am able to this moment. Tomorrow, I will come again and lay more of it at your feet. I am thankful you've chosen me to live a legacy of love. Although in turmoil, by faith I walk away from my burning rage. Please give me grace to go forward one day at a time.

Where Reality Begins

Death of a marriage is not the end of the line. You think, *He got it the way he wanted.* Even if he did, his way is not the final say-so; divorce is not the last word. If you dare, there are new directions. There are choices somewhere between wallowing in misery or going off like a fool and chasing fantasies.

C.S. Lewis said,

> Of course, we never wanted, and never asked, to be made into the sort of creatures He is going to make us into...We

must not be surprised if we are in for a rough time…God
is forcing [us] on,…putting [us] into situations where [we]
will have to be very much braver, or more patient, or more
loving, than [we] ever dreamed of being before.[1]

Where the old dream ends, a new one can begin. Only you
can do the necessary heart work. Someday you, too, will look
beyond the window and say, "I love where I'm heading." But for
now, your attention is focused on the heart work lying in your
lap. Threading the needle that will pierce the fabric and prick your
finger. Recycling what's ragged and worn into an heirloom.

*Great faith isn't the ability to believe long and far into
the misty future. It's simply taking God at his word and
taking the next step.*
—JONI EARECKSON TADA

Kari: "Don't change your tender heart and become vindictive,"
said Barney, a friend since high school. "Somebody out there is
looking for someone just like you."

Barney was right. God used rejection to recycle the remnants
of my dreams and redirect my focus. I served in our church divorce-
recovery program, began to write about hope and purpose, and
started a speaking ministry for women—and guess what?

I married a man who accepts me just as I am.

*If we go down into ourselves, we find that we possess
exactly what we desire.*
—SIMONE WEIL

Noelle: "I can't be divorced," I told my counselor early on. "I'm not made that way. I can't be a single mom." But with my cooperation, Grace began to create a quilt out of the remnants of my life. Little by little, I started enjoying what I could do, inviting friends over to fill our house, and inventing new ways to make memories.

I still can't believe it—a new person emerged. The new me is less straight, less stressed, and much more free-hearted. I still quake at life's unknowns, but an oppression has lifted that I was unaware of until, with distance, I realized it was no longer there.

On Spiritual Renewal

Kari: I tended to take on more than I could handle. Sometimes my pulse raced over 160—sitting. I kept tripping over Psalm 46:10: "Be still, and know that I am God." *And just how do I "be still" with too much to do and so much to process?* I wondered.

I discovered it meant swinging just one foot at a time off the edge of the bed instead of mindless rushing into the day. Early on, when my anger came quickly and was automatic, I determined to forgive Ed. I wanted to live my values and vision in stillness. The Lord's return gave me something to look forward to. I knew that when I stand in heaven, God won't look me over for accomplishments like a 50-year marriage—he'll be interested in my heart—whether I stayed faithful to him.

Recently, I found a slip of paper in a file from that time. It reads, "The kind of faith God values seems to develop best when everything fuzzes over, when God stays silent, when the fog rolls in... Fidelity involves learning to trust that, out beyond the perimeter of fog, God still reigns and has not abandoned us, no matter how it may appear."[2]

Noelle: At first, I couldn't pray at all. My father kept reminding me, "God didn't fail you, Noelle. Dan failed God." Later, I dressed my wounds with a short and simple liturgy I wrote myself and prayed every single morning: "Lord, take my broken pieces. That's all I have. Rearrange and put them back together in a new paradigm." I still pray that prayer, changing the things I tag onto it:

- *An affirmation*—"Noelle, I love and accept you just the way you are. I welcome happiness, love, intimacy, and prosperity into your life."
- *A homespun request*—"Eternal Grace, I want to keep a clean conscience. My desire is to be resilient and radiant at last."

I examined my life for failures and sins of omission in my marriage. It was hard. I was self-righteous. I asked the Lord to show me and forgive me, then enable me to look deeper. When faith appeared to fail, I made room for disappointment and let spiritual questions rise to the surface. These were keys to healing and growth in wisdom.

> *May the God of all grace, who called us to His eternal glory by Christ Jesus, after you have suffered a while, perfect, establish, strengthen, and settle you.*
> —1 PETER 5:10

On Emotional Refocus

Kari: I learned to live the moments before I made it through the months. In time, I discovered the peace that comes from holding everything and everyone around me loosely. I had to let go of...

- Being Ed's wife. I thought at first it was better than being alone. Divorced, I no longer fit in our couples' Sunday school class or with friends at a dinner table for six. I couldn't check "married" on official documents, conveying stability to the business world. But when I untangled my feelings, I knew I would be okay on my own.

- Our special place. Ed and I spent many weekends clearing the lot and fixing up our mountain cabin. We dreamed of retiring there, someday uniting our frantic lives. Now things are different. Richard and I blended our lives. We welcomed four dogs and two goats into our family. I walk through our wildflower garden, scattering birdseed. As I watch it cascade across the wrinkled knees of the hillside, I remind myself to live one day at a time. To embrace the moment, then let it go.

- The privacy of my emotions and stability of my values. I felt exposed when the divorce summons arrived in the mail with my name on it. That meant a file documenting the end of my marriage was in the county clerk's office, open to the public. And instead of the newspaper announcement of my twenty-fifth wedding anniversary, a divorce notice silently screamed, *Failure. And you call yourself a Christian?*

At first, I questioned what I believed about myself. Was I too serious? unattractive? unlovable? Should I slap on more makeup or lighten my hair? Study how-to-flirt books? Hit the bar scene?

Instead, I dogged God for the belonging and acceptance I so desperately craved. I bathed my mind in the Psalms and found the "right-now" way of looking at his assurances. I knew that only the Lord could redeem and stabilize my life. I prayed for courage to believe he would because he loves me and treasures a pure heart, a gentle spirit, and honesty.

When Melanie spent weekends with Ed, I learned to relish a quiet, empty house as I stretched out on the couch with a book and classical music. But there were times I had to will myself to be content in the moment.

I faced my fear of public humiliation and shame by talking about divorce to friends and family. Each time I encountered another divorcée, I was overwhelmed with compassion and hugged her as if to say, *I know your anguish, and I care.*

Noelle: As a divorcée-to-be, I cried the entire first two meetings in a recovery group. My wound was raw. I felt I'd had the worst experience of anyone present there—until a young woman joined. She'd just found out her best friend's baby had been fathered by her soon-to-be-ex-husband. Before my divorce, I would have thought, *How do people get themselves into messes like that?* Now, I knew humiliation like that can come out of nowhere.

In my first efforts to rise above my own pain, I told myself, *Get out of bed. Kiss the children. Buy milk.* Next: *Cry when you feel like it. Think beautiful. Make room for whimsy.*

But it got harder. I wanted to allow love a place, so I faced down destructive patterns. To break the cycle of hateful thoughts engulfing me, I learned to change the way I felt about the bad things.

I set a goal to see the truth, not the lies, in what happened. Instead of allowing myself to think, *Betrayed...ripped off...trashed,* I trained myself to view things from a larger perspective. The Neighbor did me a favor by forcing Dan's infidelities into the light. He lost the precious things: a good wife, beautiful home, and his family.

My negative emotions toward him eventually neutralized. I no longer feel hate or love. Perhaps with time, I'll feel friendly. I rest in the fact there is a time for everything and I don't have to force it. I have a right to emotional boundaries while I'm healing.

> *You don't know where the wind will blow...You don't know what God is doing...Plant early in the morning, and work until evening, because you don't know if this or that will succeed. They might both do well.*
> —ECCLESIASTES 11:5,6 NCV

On Practical Recycle

Kari: Accepting my new role was a critical decision. I risked turning scary corners and embracing a changing me. I found I could do...

- Simple things I'd never tried before. Caulking the bathtub, pouring concrete in driveway cracks, painting the fence, and climbing on the roof to inspect shingles. I was rewarded with the pride of accomplishment.

- Big things I'd never done before. I handled insurance paperwork after an automobile accident, including estimates, repairs, and car rental; qualified for a mortgage; and purchased my own home.

- Incredible things I'd never imagined. Ignoring Ed's harassing letters and phone calls, responding in a strictly-business fashion. Giving up my right to vindicate myself when I learned what he was saying about me. "Truth needs no defense," I told myself and others, deciding other people could believe what they wanted and I would not waste energy trying to change their opinion.

- Beautiful things with so little. Remodeling memories, I splashed my home with light and color—peachy tones and splotches of apple green and sky blue. Ed was welcome to the black-vinyl look he took with him. Instead of crying over the garden I'd lost, I bought two redwood boxes for my patio, planted seeds, picked off snails, and then pampered my home with sweet-scented bouquets.

I learned I was not alone. The first evening I stood in the doorway of a divorce-recovery class, I felt embarrassed and ashamed. Later, I realized my fears were the same as everyone else's in that room. Soon I made friends and started a monthly potluck. I helped with the church single-again group, volunteered for leadership, and became a speaker.

Noelle: I began to accept, even embrace, the changes turning my life upside down—the divorce and my reduced circumstances. I used the momentum of blessing to initiate change. This is what I did:

- Painted our front door hunter green.
- Hung a shiny brass porch lamp in place of a clunky old black one.
- Planted a baby maple tree in my front lawn to mark my passage into the new.
- Redecorated empty spots on the walls with other pictures and photos.
- Lost 20 pounds and enjoyed the compliments.
- Invested in a fabulous eye cream.
- Cleaned out closets and gave 50 bags and boxes to charity.
- Took a bunch of clothes to a resale shop, earning $$ for two new outfits.
- Welcomed an exchange student into our home. Presto, I had four daughters!
- When I started buying shoes again, I went for high heels to give me a lift.

Whatever happens that breaks us open to a deeper invasion of the Lord's spirit is a blessing in disguise. Whenever we face difficulties and problems that break our willfulness or arrogant control of our lives, it is a gift.

—LLOYD JOHN OGILVIE

I Like This New Me

Handmade heirlooms are rich gifts. Whether quilted, crocheted, embroidered, or tatted, every stitch contains a thought. Even strips of threadbare clothing can be braided into a beautifully patterned rug. When your fingers travel across the ridges of Grandmother's afghan neatly folded across your bed, you trace the mind of its creator.

So it is with the leftover fabric of your life. God works with the dark and light threads to weave an original. The patterns take on personality as the textures change. The loose, tangled threads will one day be straightened and tucked. In cold nights to come, you will snuggle beneath a legacy of years: scraps of yesterday, spares of today, swatches of tomorrow, safe and warm.

Even on days when you hide under the covers, like the psalmist you can say, "When I awake, I am still with You."[3]

Are you made of sturdy stuff? Are you creative? inventive? resourceful?

You are all of the above. It is God in you, the hope of glory.

P.S.—You're beautiful!

My Hope Is Increasing

What visual thing might I do to take an active step toward positive change?

- Get a new haircut or hair color?
- Start a small garden plot?
- Give the walls of my home a fabulous new coat of paint?

Here are ten things it would be possible for me to change this month:

1.

2.

3.

4.

5.

6.

7.

8.

9.

10.

All the Comforts of Home

Tuck seasonal indulgences into your lifestyle:

Spring:

- Rise early and walk before breakfast. Look for firsts: the first crocus, the first robin, the first leaves.
- Buy the latest nail polish and a new pair of open-toe shoes.
- Write a letter to yourself about new dreams. Seal it in a self-addressed, stamped envelope and ask a friend to mail it to you in one year.

Summer:

- Grow mint in a pot for use in salads, iced tea, and lemonade. Freeze it in ice cubes for use in winter stews, marinades, and hot teas.
- Relax outside (with sunscreen) for a few minutes each day. Listen for summer sounds and smells. Document them in your journal.
- Take down heavy drapes and decorations in your home. Enjoy the uncluttered space.

Autumn:

- Go on a seed-catalog tour for bulbs with a mug of hot apple cider. Sitting by your fireside, envision next spring's colors.
- Bundle up and stroll along a beach or through a park on a windy day.
- Join a choir or the circus! This is the season to make new friends.

Winter:

- Invest in a box of scented candles. Light them in the late afternoon and keep them glowing all evening.

- Invite a friend to have coffee with you at a place neither of you has been.
- Make a list of books you want to read. Put several on reserve at the library and see how many you'll read before spring comes again.

Chapter Six

I Need Time to Feel
So I Can Heal

There is a right time for everything:
…a time to cry
…a time to grieve
…a time for scattering stones
…a time not to hug
…a time to lose
…a time to tear
…a time to be quiet
…a time for hating.

—ECCLESIASTES 3:1-8 TLB

⁓ꙮ⁓

Kari: "You're from tough pioneer stock," my mother had said as I hopped aboard that westbound train. At 18, I'd courageously packed my trunk with well-folded ideals and vivid dreams. In midlife, embarking on singleness again, I lugged the heavy baggage that goes with a divorce—now filled with rumpled ideals and faded dreams.

I wondered, *Will anyone ever love me again, so steeped in anxiety and seething with rage? Was Ed right when he called me crazy and left me?* Unable to straighten my disheveled emotions about Ed's rejection, I worried about losing what little courage remained. When I needed to focus on a new direction, I couldn't focus at all.

One evening after work, I went back to our former home to pay rent due for the time I'd lived there after escrow closed while searching for a place of my own. My heart pumped wildly as I walked up the steps and rang the bell. I wrote my check to the new owner, then quickly drove off. It was agonizing to see a different family living there.

Several miles down the road, I felt uneasy. After pulling over to the curb, I switched on the dashboard light to double-check my figures. Feeling the stare of every passing motorist, I recalculated and finally arrived at the same total twice. *I've written that check for a couple hundred dollars too much!* Embarrassed, I returned to say I'd made a mistake. I felt humiliated. Annoyed. Vulnerable. *Am I going crazy?*

No. I was going through a divorce.

My mind told me I was an intelligent, stable, responsible woman. But my confidence was sinking. I was physically exhausted and emotionally overwhelmed. I had been spiritually shaken. When I discovered a pile of bank statements pushed to the back of my desk, I admitted I was coming mentally unglued. I felt like the overturned truck and trailer I'd recently seen on a busy highway near my home. The remains and contents were scattered across the grassy divider.

Had the driver survived? I wondered. *Will I?*

> *Anyone who believes that God guarantees a successful marriage to every Christian is in for a shock.*
> —DR. JAMES DOBSON

Where Do I Start?

Divorce victims look a lot like that overturned truck and trailer. Upside down. Sprawled across the divider of past and present while curiosity seekers watch from the side. *What happened to your marriage?* they seem to say through a glance or a nod. Few take the initiative to ask, "What is happening to you?" Most are waiting for the scene to be cleaned up and the wreck relegated to the past so everyone can get on with their lives. Some say plainly, "Get over it."

Bewildered, you wonder, *Where do I start?* The landscape before you is spattered with the lifeblood of lost love. Only you know how much you have lost: a companion. Family. Your identity as somebody's wife. Hope. Purpose. Friends. Face. Maybe your faith. Only you feel the pain of picking through the fragments. Only you know the agony of walking away from precious things and feeling that your mind and body may end up as shattered as your heart.

The degree of shock and numbness you experience depends upon the severity of your injury. The more the dream meant to you, the closer your attachment—the deeper the wound. The more you invested in the man and the relationship, the heavier your losses. Shock numbs the pain for a while. But shock wears off. Eventually, you feel.

And feel you must. Never be afraid to feel honest emotion, because that is where healing begins.

"Accepting reality translates into a specific skill with predictable physiological and emotional results," says Barbara Lang Stern. "The loss sinks in…Your thoughts are concerned with wanting things to be different and, in response, your brain starts firing messages (which you experience as feelings) that something is wrong."

Quoting Gary Emery, PhD, director of the Los Angeles Center for Cognitive Therapy, Stern says, "'As long as you don't accept the messages, your brain keeps sending them to you. Your alternative to resisting reality is to make a conscious decision to accept the existing situation, including the fact that you're distressed by it...' Acceptance is the first step, not a last..."[1]

> *There are times in life when each of us, no matter how mature and well, is frankly unglued. We need to...simply allow ourselves the clumsiness and awkwardness of being hurt and untogether.*
> —Dr. Alla Renee Bozarth

No Wonder It Hurts So Much

The aftermath of divorce, like debris left behind at an accident scene, is not predictable or uniform. Tear apart a piece of paper. You end up with two uneven, ragged edges. Part of the left side remains with the right side and vice versa. Divorce rips your most intimate spiritual, physical, emotional, and mental bonds. Part of who you are remains with your former spouse, and part of who he is stays with you. No wonder it hurts so much.

When you admit and accept the pain of this separation, you validate the biblical standard for the sanctity and sacrament of marriage: two people becoming *one flesh*. Divorce sounds and smells like torn flesh. No wonder God hates it.[2] He created man in his image, then said, "It is not good that man should be alone."[3] Marriage represents the relationship between Christ and the church.[4] This mystery of attachment created in marriage is one of God's best ideas.

John Townsend, clinical psychologist, asserts that "attachment or bondedness is our deepest need...It means letting others inside the private vulnerable parts of ourselves…It occurs when we take the risk to allow someone else to matter enough to us to hurt us if they choose to."[5]

Brenda Hunter, author of *Beyond Divorce*, says, "Possibly no marital act affects the self-esteem as deeply as having a spouse choose someone else to love. I do not care whether the involvement is emotional or sexual or both. The fact remains that I, the wife, am in some area of my life found wanting…What I valued, what I believed, were obviously insignificant…What I was, was simply not enough."

Hunter writes further, "Affairs don't just happen. They are willed into existence. Prior to the affair, there is a deliberate turning away from the spouse and a willful search for another person."[6]

The pain you experience after rejection is a bold message about the fundamental importance of attachment. Many counselors claim that, for every four years of marriage, healing can take one year. But time itself does not restore. Time is a tool God uses to move you through the moments, days, weeks, and years of life. Time is the dimension within which you heal, a gift of room and space where change can occur.

In the beginning, the best choice you can make is to choose to accept what has happened to you and embrace it. The pain will not last forever.

At times, when the pain is most intense, there is nothing but to merely try keeping sane and alive one more day. At other times, when the hurting is not so excruciating, it actually sharpens the senses. There are moments for discovering what otherwise cannot be easily learned.

—AUTHOR UNKNOWN

Noelle: At first, Dan communicated to his family and friends that our divorce was a mutual agreement, and he procrastinated filing. Did he want to be able to say I initiated the final split? He implied to me in front of a witness that he would stay married if I accepted his mistresses.

After we separated, Dan agreed to marriage counseling. During that period he bought a birthday present for The Neighbor on our joint credit card and belittled me for "overreacting" when the fact he slept with her came to light. Our counselor laid a hand on his shoulder. "Dan, you're not giving this a chance," he said. "If you decide to make your marriage work, call and make another appointment, and let's talk about it with Noelle." Dan never called him back.

I had trusted Dan. I believed in his sincerity. But when his pretense was exposed, my pain quotient went off the chart. He twisted my anger back against me. "There! You see? I can't be married to an angry woman."

But my anger at Dan was nothing compared to the rage I hurled against myself. "How could I have been so naive?" I asked another counselor. "Was I wrong to trust him all these years?"

"No," she replied. "Trust is the gift you are supposed to give your spouse. You did the right thing. The problem was, he wasn't worthy of it."

Little by little I learned that trusting my negative feelings—guilt, anger, and sadness—would bring me insight, comfort, and energy as I interpreted their messages.

Anger is such a healthy emotion; I didn't feel enough of it. So therefore, I felt more pain as guilt. Low self-esteem took over.

—ARLENE SOMERVILLE

Forever Changed

Sometimes you wish you could turn off the feelings. Push a button. Poof! Anger and anguish disappear. You long to escape because it hurts too much. Some nights, the only way you can fall asleep is to daydream yourself into an exotic world where stars are warm on a dark night and ocean foam is like a caressing cashmere blanket.

But morning comes soon enough. In the face of desperation, a kind of raw courage rises to the surface. You realize, *If I weren't angry, then something would be wrong.*

In certain situations, rage may be the only appropriate response. Karl Miller, a marriage and family therapist at Covenant Psychological Services in Redwood City, California, says, "Anger can be used two ways. To separate and get in touch with our boundaries, or as a way to keep the other person involved with us." Miller, a former pastor who remarried after divorce, believes some relationships are *hostile–dependent.* "Anger is a way to hang on to a relationship," he says.[7]

When you rant, "How could you do this to me?" it may prevent you from detaching emotionally. Okay, you make mistakes expressing rage. Don't beat yourself up. You rage because you loved. In the sinkholes of destructive emotions, a higher love can fan flames of forgiveness. You will learn ways to allow this fire to empower you. How? Do you pretend it will go away? Kick the dog? Shop it off? Blame yourself, then reach for the cookie jar? Decide all men are jerks? How do you detach without losing more of yourself in the process?

Archibald Hart, former dean of the Graduate School of Psychology and professor at Fuller Theological Seminary in Pasadena, California, says to confront painful feelings and move beyond them.[8]

Giving yourself permission to feel love, then anger—and each emotion in between—may appear to spiral you backward and downward. It doesn't. To *feel* is to be alive. Feelings help you live rooted in the here and now and remember why you got here. Pain provides clues to truth as you peel away the layers of loss. Feelings make you human. Feelings also make you more like Jesus.

"God used Hosea's unhappy story to illustrate his own whipsaw emotions," writes Philip Yancey. "As Israel broke his trust again and again, he was forced to endure the awful shame of a wounded lover." He notes that God's tone is close to self-pity: "I am like a moth to Ephraim, like rot to the people of Judah."

Yancey continues, "God seems to 'change his mind' every few seconds...He is preparing to obliterate Israel—wait, now he is weeping, holding out open arms—no, he is sternly pronouncing judgment again. These shifting moods seem hopelessly irrational except to anyone who has been jilted by a lover."[9]

Divorce Changes How You Look at Life

- You lose your innocence but gain discernment.
- You learn when you feel, you heal.
- You realize rejection can't define you unless you allow it to.
- You accept that reality sometimes hurts like crazy but sets you free.

Talk About Tears

Our Creator made us, in his wisdom and in his image, with the capacity for love, anger, and jealousy; joy, sadness, and hurt. He respects these emotions. The psalmist exclaimed, "A broken... heart—these, O God, you will not despise."[10] Jesus promised,

"Blessed are those who mourn."[11] The apostle Mark records that Christ's last excruciating breath was preceded by a loud cry.

God built healing right into heartbreak. He created tear ducts so we can weep. William Frey is a biochemist who is both a researcher at Health Partners St. Paul–Ramsey Medical Center and a professor at the University of Minnesota. For much of his career, he has been fascinated by a question few other scientists have asked: Why do we cry?

"I wanted to understand how humans alleviate stress," he says in the *Parade* magazine article "Go Ahead, Cry" by Michael Ryan. Frey found that "the only physiological mechanism we've evolved to [alleviate stress] that is different from every other animal is the ability to cry emotional tears."[12]

> *The darkest hour is only 60 minutes.*
> —AUTHOR UNKNOWN

Frey discovered that 85 percent of women and 73 percent of men felt better after they had shed tears in a stressful situation. People are less angry and less sad after crying, he found, because tears carry to the brain a unique combination of stress-relieving chemicals at a level 30 times higher than that in the blood, including endorphins (painkilling hormones produced after physical exercise) and prolactin (a hormone that helps nursing mothers produce milk).[13]

So, go ahead and cry your eyes out. Wail your gut-splintering rage to the heavens. Know that the Holy Spirit grieves along with you, even for you, in groans that cannot be uttered, according to the will of God. Scripture is full of talk about tears. Jesus wept when a friend died. God himself cries and weeps. In the new heaven, God will wipe away every tear. Jesus was not embarrassed or offended by the woman who washed his feet with her tears. He honors and even "bottles" our precious tears.[14] Shed bucketsful!

Where there's pain, there's still feeling. When there's feeling, there's hope. A time is coming "to laugh…to dance… for gathering stones…to hug…to find…to repair…to speak up…for loving."[15] You will be forever changed by your willingness to confront and embrace your pain.

> *Sometimes even muscle cannot substitute for tears.*
> —PAUL SIMON

The Darker Side of Feelings

Truth. Goodness. Love. We use these words lightly but know so little about them. We're afraid to think or talk about their counterparts. Yet residing within each of us is both the good and the bad of our humanity. Divorce brings to the surface what we have trouble admitting even to ourselves. Another authentic element of feeling-to-heal is encountering the shadow side within ourselves.

Kari: I remember the day I no longer loved Ed. One Friday afternoon, he came to pick up Melanie at the house I'd just moved into. It was two months before our divorce was final. As he stood on the porch, I thought back to the day I promised to love him for a lifetime, my vision clear-cut and defined. Now my eyes traced his face, and I wondered what I had seen in him. How could I have slept with him? What had I trusted? Why? Truth blew me away as forcefully as the harsh December wind had ripped off the roof of my garden shelter.

I stared past the facade of the man I had loved into the face of my betrayer. The man who was once my husband was now a stranger. I hardly recognized this person who knew me well enough to wound me. Because I had given him intimate access, he knew the buttons to push to confuse and humiliate me. On the front porch that day, I felt naked.

Isn't that how Adam and Eve saw each other after they feasted on the forbidden fruit? Stripped of innocence. Seeing good and evil. Tasting death. Naked.

I closed the door and lingered behind the window curtains. As if in a theater watching a movie about somebody else's life, I watched Ed and his girlfriend drive away with our daughter. Later, my pencil stabbed the word *hate* into a page of my journal. I knew I was looking back at Eden. I'd been disrobed. My rose-colored glasses had been ripped away. That day I stared into my own potential for darkness.

Man is the only animal that laughs and cries, because he is the only one that can see the difference between the way things are and the way they ought to be.
—WILLIAM HAZLITT

Noelle: One evening I sat in front of a fire, surrounded by my children and a couple of their friends. We were watching an inspiring video and, in that brief respite, I was savoring hope.

During the climax of the movie, Dan walked through the front door without knocking, right in front of the TV, and into my bedroom. I stared, flabbergasted. Just as quickly, he left. Minutes later I found an envelope lying on my pillow, addressed with the nickname he used to call me. Surprised, I thought it might contain some positive sentiment.

How wrong I was! I quickly skimmed through a detailed list of denouncements of my shortcomings. The words and insults of the man before whom I'd bared body and soul jabbed viciously at my femininity. This was the only man I'd ever slept with. I had borne his children. He'd promised to cherish and honor me. I was horrified at his cruelty, apparently calculated to hit me just before sleep.

Though it was midnight, I made up my mind. I would find a gun—somewhere, anywhere—take it to his apartment, and be done with him.

The problem was, I didn't know where to get a gun. I called a friend instead, livid with murderous thoughts. She kept talking until I was calmer. Then one of my daughters came in and sat beside me on the bed. Her childlike ability to see plainly was like a balm to my spirit. She said without malice, "Mommy, it's like the devil entered into Daddy and is speaking through him." But I had seen something even more threatening—the evil in me.

The next day, Dan called to apologize for the note. But I felt knocked down and thrown off guard again. Later I was able to discern the pattern he typically used—disarming me with blame or shame, then appealing to my sensitivity or spirituality. Feeling jerked around, I saw my hurt evolving into hate.

> *Sometimes, there just aren't enough rocks.*
> —Winston Groom, *Forrest Gump*

Calling It What It Is

"Evil is real," says M. Scott Peck in *The Road Less Traveled*. "It is not the figment of the imagination of a primitive religious mind feebly attempting to explain the unknown." Peck writes that those who respond to goodness with evil do so without "conscious malice but blindly, lacking awareness of their own evil, indeed seeking to avoid any such awareness. [They]...hate the light because it reveals themselves to themselves. They will destroy the light, the goodness, the love in order to avoid the pain of such self-awareness."[16]

Peck defines evil not as *nonlove* (ordinary laziness) but as *antilove.*

Divorce's worst-case scenarios are not just "we don't love each other anymore," or cases of incompatibility—the lazy nonlove Peck refers to. In worst-case scenarios there is a profoundly deceptive element functioning under a facade of "goodness." Deceivers deny real feelings (love or hate) and refuse to validate the feelings of others. They can't. The act of feeling, reflecting, or examining the consequences of their feelings, words, or deeds is too threatening.

But that is exactly what people of integrity have to do. There is no alternative but to turn the tables upside down just as Jesus did in the temple. Do the opposite of what the deceiver expects, what he will not do for himself. Accept the consequences of self-awareness—your sin, your own capacity for antilove. Confess it. Grieve it. Ask God's forgiveness. Only such a bold step of holding tightly to the truth breaks the destructive power of evil.

If a thing is free to be good, it is also free to be bad... Because free will, though it makes evil possible, is also the only thing that makes possible any love or goodness or joy worth having.

—C.S. LEWIS

The Good Grief

You are an average woman. You married an ordinary man. You didn't expect wealth, fame, or luxury. You just wanted to love, be loved, and raise a family with a husband in mutual support, faith, and fidelity. You longed for emotional intimacy in marriage. Like us, you are not perfect. You make mistakes. Perhaps he used your imperfection to justify his leaving.

Now you are examining the good, the bad, and the truth about the man you loved. And about yourself. The truth is that part of you still loves him. In a deep place beyond tears, you cry some days—but not just mourning what you've lost. Though you grieve that your love, sensuality, and best years were spent with an unworthy man, you mourn his loss, too. You wonder if he'll ever face the truth and make the choice to open his own wounds to healing, to feel his feelings, or to talk to somebody about his issues and choice to act out.

Grief is about coming to terms with what could have been (a good marriage) while thrusting your fist at what is (divorce). Your loss includes both the bad and good parts of the marriage. To grieve is to go back and take inventory of what is gone and what remains. Grief immobilizes you. It acts like the lead drape thrown across your body at the dentist's office. It is God's way of slowing you down when your soul has work to do. *Gravare* is Latin for "to burden," and *gravis* means "heavy." Jesus said, "Come to me, all you who labor and are heavy laden."[17]

"God's solution for resolving your loss of relationships, dreams, ideals, and opportunities is sadness," says Dr. John Townsend. "Rather than something to be avoided, this sadness, or grief, allows you to let go of what you cannot have in order to make room in your heart for what you can have."[18] Sadness does a job.

> *One of the sadder aspects of a good marriage gone bad is that there are so many pleasant memories to go with the nightmares.*
> —BARBARA COCHRAN BERRY
> (FORMER WIFE OF O.J. SIMPSON'S TRIAL ATTORNEY)

Kari: Divorce didn't shut me down. It got my attention. For too long my feelings had been invalidated by Ed and denied by me. As I look back on those last two years we were together, I realize I was knitting away at what was already unraveling. A friend observed that toward the end I was more in love with the marriage than the man. I wish you could read my journal entries about the weekends Ed and I spent at our cabin. I labeled it "Our Family's Journey to Sanctuary," but only the brief final entry, documenting our last Thanksgiving together, says anything real: "November 27. *My heart is heavy.*"

> *Not everything that is faced can be changed, but nothing can be changed until it is faced.*
> —JAMES BALDWIN

Hope's Wake-up Call

Grieving can begin in your spirit even before you know what you are grieving about. You can be numbed by a mate's lack of response to love even before you suspect unfaithfulness. The numbness is sometimes simply defined in psychological jargon as "denial," but the issue is really complex, spiritually speaking. Striving to think no evil, bear and believe all things, hope and endure all things, you tuck the issue to bed. You hope "against hope" that things will get better. But even hope meets its match when it encounters truth. "Hope deferred makes the heart sick," says Proverbs.[19] When hope is continuously delayed or denied, the only appropriate response is grief.

> *It is possible to create light and sound and order within,*
> *no matter what calamity may befall us in the outer world.*
> —HELEN KELLER

Your Downside Will Be Up Again

Be patient with yourself. Listen to your heart and honor it. The writer of Proverbs compared the heart to a reflection that reveals the person you are when no one is looking.[20] Let God take his time healing you. Expect delays and detours. Stop beating yourself up because you can't avoid roadblocks or potholes on the way through divorce.

Always remember how far the Lord has brought you and that your journey is not over yet. You'll never forget the pain; but someday you'll say, "I'm a better person because of what I've gone through. My heart is more tender. My interior life, richer."

Jacque Klippenes, a professional counselor in Castro Valley, California, says, "The key is to understand that God designed us with a tremendous capacity for transparency and vulnerability to live in a world that was innocent. He didn't design us to experience the psychic trauma that may have happened, that kind of hurt. Sin is a phenomenal assault on the mind and heart."

"This is the pay-dirt reality," adds Jacque's husband, Jeff, also a counselor. "But into that reality, Christ comes, saying 'I will walk with you guys as flesh. I will feel what you feel, and I think I can help you make sense out of this.' Then it becomes more of a *Columbo* mystery, where we begin to play the role of sleuth. We start dogging God, saying, 'Okay. You love me, speak to me about this puzzle. How am I to get empowerment out of this?'"

Jacque urges counseling clients to appreciate the full spectrum of emotion in a divorce: "We get our most reflective understanding when we're hurting, depressed, broken, sad, or angry. At these times, the human soul is most open and available to God."

"Yes," says Jeff, "when God is allowed access to our pain, when we allow the Holy Spirit to energize us, we move forward one step at a time."[21]

> *Though nothing can bring back the hour*
> *Of splendor in the grass, of glory in the flower;*
> *We will grieve not, rather find*
> *Strength in what remains behind;*
> *In the primal sympathy*
> *Which having been must ever be;*
> *In the soothing thoughts that spring*
> *Out of human suffering...*
>
> —WILLIAM WORDSWORTH

I Need Time to Feel So I Can Heal

Great achievers often suffer greatly. Ask yourself,

- How might I make the world richer once I've gone through this present distress?

- What am I learning about myself?

- What three qualities do I most like about myself?

Chapter Seven

I Am Giving Myself a Chance

*He who dwells in the shelter of the Most High will rest in
the shadow of the Almighty.*

—PSALM 91:1 NIV

⎯ৎ৯⎯

All girls are princesses," Sara told the boarding-school principal.
"No matter how poor or ragged or alone; all girls are princesses—
didn't *your* father ever tell you that?"

In one moving scene of the 1995 film version of Frances
Hodgson Burnett's *A Little Princess*, Sara is told her father is dead
and she is destitute and unwanted. She is taken from her own
birthday party, dressed in rags, and led to the dark attic.

Alone, in shock, uprooted from everything she knew to be true
and beautiful, Sara slips to the dirty, damp floor. Spying a piece
of chalk, she draws a circle around herself and curls up inside it,
weeping, "Papa! Papa! Papa!…" She wants to believe the circle is
her safe place, within which no evil can penetrate.

A real circle of protection is often mentioned in God's Word:
the shadow of his wings, our refuge and fortress, the secret places
of the cliff, a strong tower, our hiding place.[1]

At times, our heavenly Father becomes the God who hides himself.[2] In times of loss, fear, and despair, we find our way to this circle that contains our broken dreams. It is a safe place. A place to grieve and reflect.

God says, "I will give you the treasures of darkness and hidden riches of secret places."[3] All girls are princesses. Like Sara, we too are motivated by what our Father told us. We recognize our calling in spite of evidence to the contrary. We move to bless the world by living out that calling based not on circumstances, but on who we know ourselves to be and whose we are.

> *Courage doesn't always roar. Sometimes courage is the quiet voice at the end of the day saying, "I will try again tomorrow."*
>
> —M.A. HERSHEY

The Safe Place and Beyond

Divorce isolates. Like the little princess, you feel cut off from the familiar, engulfed in circumstances you can't control. You can't imagine the shadow encircling you is a safe place. To dwell in shelter means you rest in shadow. You can't believe you'll ever regroup and step beyond it. But you will.

Noelle: My former position in publishing was a ringside seat to women's pain. Thousands of letters, manuscripts, and testimonies convinced me that the traditional mode of relating to each other in the church is sadly ineffectual. Human hurt is holy, not something to be hidden away behind a Sunday mask.

The publication I worked for initiated a page of letters, promising readers their personal stories would be listened to and their pain honored, not patronized. Each issue, my task included reading dozens of letters and selecting the few to print. I often leaned over my desk, tears dripping onto hand-penned lines. Without conscious knowing, I was already within this circle of women, grieving for what was yet to happen to me.

At a writers' conference, I spoke about breaking through artificial spiritual taboos, though with discretion. Urging writers to go beyond conventional boundaries, I argued for transparency and vulnerability.

A year later, my own courage was tested. I was scheduled to teach again, and no one knew of my divorce. Would I admit the truth, trusting that my pain would now be embraced as holy? I decided not to maintain emotional distance behind my professional facade.

One writer, taking courage from my talk the previous year, had brought an article proposal on her divorce. I listened, intending to offer rewriting tips. As she elaborated on her manuscript, finally my emotions collapsed. "Kari," I said, stopping her, "I'm going through this same thing right now." I looked into her bright eyes. "But I want to be like you. I want the twinkle back."

From that moment, we spoke as sisters. Kari's life affirmed my desire to survive and heal. Her story was published, followed by appreciative letters from other thankful readers. That is how this book was born. By drawing me and others into her circle of experience, she became a safe place, validating my pain and encouraging the move beyond it.

The steadfast love of the LORD never ceases, his mercies never come to an end; they are new every morning.
—LAMENTATIONS 3:23 RSV

Kari: After Ed moved out, I sensed an invisible shield encircling me about an arm's length from my body. I felt protected within its circumference, although each day brought further confirmation of Ed's affairs. I picked up the sword of the Spirit before bedtime, circling Scripture verses and jotting thoughts in the margins. "Direct my steps by Your word," I prayed with the psalmist, "and let no iniquity have dominion over me."[4]

One day on a job, my fingers froze. My mind was flooded with graphic images of Ed with another woman. Then I remembered, "Thou wilt keep him in perfect peace, whose mind is stayed on thee,"[5] a verse I'd memorized as a child. My mind cleared; I resumed my work. The sword had severed the images.

From that day on, whenever I needed to have my thoughts cleared, I repeated that verse—at first in its entirety. Eventually, "Thou wilt" was sufficient to allow me to get on with my job. In the middle of the night, when I couldn't silence my pounding chest or still the tapes spinning in my brain, I knelt beside my bed and used the sword to banish demons.

Here, within this place of safety, I discovered the process I now call "turnabout thinking."

Turnabout Thinking

Divorce's most brutal battles are fought in the mind. They are about what is true and what is not. Turnabout thinking clarifies what can't be changed and what can. It discriminates between fact and fiction. When your worth is attacked or belief system assaulted, how you define what happens to you determines whether you see opportunities or obstacles, challenges or catastrophes.

Eugene Peterson paraphrased a portion of Paul's letter to the Ephesians like this: "It's in Christ that we find out who we are and what we are living for. Long before we first heard of Christ and got our hopes up, he had his eye on us, had designs on us for glorious living, part of the overall purpose he is working out in everything and everyone."[6]

The apostle Paul said, "We have the mind of Christ."[7] Becoming empowered through the mind of Christ is what turnabout thinking is all about. It is choosing to think in terms congruent with what God's designs for you are all about and with his plan for glorious living.

> *Everything can be taken from us but one thing—the last of the human freedoms—to choose one's attitude in any given circumstance.*
>
> —VICTOR FRANKL

What Do I Want? What Do I Need?

Kari: What you want and what you need are not the same thing. Only you know the difference. At least, that's what Melanie's godmother told me when she handed me a legal-sized yellow tablet and said, "Go to it." Thanks to her, I put pen to paper.

I headed for my wants and listed several intangibles like "respect" and other answers listed below. When I looked at the need list, I figured, *Okay, basic survival.* Finally, I realized I could live without my wants but not without my needs. My wants comprise contributions to my life; needs such as hope, peace, and what is eternal, affect who I am at the core of my being. Soon I was on a roll. You will be, too. Go to it!

Wants vs. Needs

Make two lists side by side (one may be longer) of everything that you want right now and everything that you need right now.

What I Want (Kari's sample answers)	What I Need (Kari's sample answers)
encouragement	shelter
respect	food
honesty	belonging
empathy	spiritual strength
freedom to fail and	hope
still be accepted	peace
to know how it feels	conversation
to have someone else	exercise
there for me	laughter

A joyful heart makes a cheerful face...Bright eyes gladden the heart.

—PROVERBS 15:13,30 NASB

Define Fact vs. Fiction

Physicians claim optimistic people are less susceptible to depression and illness.[8] They say feelings of helplessness, hopelessness, or both cause the brain to manufacture hormones that weaken the immune system. Before any such studies were published, the writer of Proverbs said, "The spirit of a man will sustain him in sickness, but who can bear a broken spirit?"[9]

A way to stay optimistic and gain back control of your emotions is to distinguish between fact and fiction in your divorce. See the truth in black-and-white. For example, if you are agonizing over your children enjoying fun-filled weekends with the other parent while labeling you the "do-your-homework-feed-the-cat-empty-the-trash mom," this exercise will help clarify your responsibility and maximize your objectivity.

Fact or Fiction

Write side-by-side lists: *Facts About My Marriage* and *Fiction About My Marriage*. Do the same about your children and about your ex. Define and hold onto what is good. Discover it was not all bad.

Facts About My Marriage (Kari's sample answers)

- Seventeen years were good.
- I enjoyed the cabin for two-and-a-half years.
- I did too much for Ed.

- Divorce could be a new beginning.

Fiction About My Marriage (Kari's sample answers)

- All twenty-two years were bad.
- The cabin was a mistake.

- I could have done more to save my marriage.
- My life is ruined by the divorce.

Facts About My Children (Kari's sample answers)

- I am doing the best I can for my daughter.
- In joint custody she'll observe inconsistencies between lifestyles.
- Our relationship is strained.

- By giving her up to God, I reduce her dad's control of me through her.

Fiction About My Children (Kari's sample answers)

- I am the only one who can help my daughter.
- It's all her dad's fault.

- Changes that I make to please her will help our relationship.
- I could have done more to make things better for her.

Facts About My Ex (Kari's sample answers)	Fiction About My Ex (Kari's sample answers)
• He lies and manipulates.	• Appealing to his conscience gets me somewhere.
• He is jealous of how I kept my life in order.	• Being depressed over him is worth the effort.
• He has committed multiple adulteries.	• Mentally rewriting the past into perfect scenes helps me.

> *Any man can fight the battle for just one day. It is only when you and I add the burden of those two awful eternities, yesterday and tomorrow, that we tremble.*
>
> —JOHN MAXWELL

Redefine Your Life

Divorce forces you to release many ideals in search of what is real. You look long and hard for bedrock values and a new direction because you desperately want to live and move on. You begin to understand the most important word about going through divorce is the word *through*. It carries you like a raft over the current tormented thoughts and the grief threatening to overwhelm. Other times, you traverse rough terrain on foot. Six milestones identify your passage as you make choices that redefine dreams and circumstances.

Milestone 1: Own What Is Real

At some point you finally decide, *If there is an experience in front of me, I will own it.* Although you hate the scar this crisis will leave, the good thing is you are addressing—or dressing—the wound. You are not denying or running from it. You stare your greatest fear in the face and acknowledge, *Yes, this is really happening to me.*

From that moment on, you move forward.

Noelle: Trying to resolve what I didn't understand, I turned over my questions like puzzle pieces. *Had I done something terrible to deserve this? Why hadn't my faith helped save our marriage? How could the heavenly Father I'd believed since childhood have let me go on trusting Dan through 20 years of infidelity? How could I bear the failure of a broken family and divorce? Could I ever believe again that all things work together for good to those who love God?*

I had to admit I was a participant in allowing the space between Dan and me to grow. I kept tolerating his move away from emotional and physical intimacy, hoping and believing that giving the gift of space and trust would turn things around. I had accepted too little, overlooked too much, and carried buckets much too small to the well of prayer. Finally, I realized that faith allows mercy to do its job, but faith can't control other people's choices. God, in his mercy, gave Dan year after year until God said, "Enough is enough."

I read about Gerald Sittser, who lost his wife, mother, and daughter in an automobile accident and said, "I absorbed the loss into my life like soil receives decaying matter until it becomes part of who I am."[10] As he was, I'm fertilized by the experience. I am enduring with dignity. I look people in the eye and am proud of my daughters who have bravely borne their share.

When I examine dreams available to me, it's clear I most want what I always did: to be the wife of a beautiful godly man and to serve God together. Each day I choose to believe Grace is still on the job, working what I can't see. If I am to remain single, each year brings a remarkable realization of the advantages of that. To be a poised single woman who is passionate about her interests, and who is confidently pursuing a new purpose, is a lovely—and quite amazing—thing to be!

Milestone 2: Let Go of What Isn't Real

Some of what you always believed just isn't true. Like a fog lifting, illusions vaporize. You feel confused, and you rage against the injustice of it all. You are in a battle to let go of a person and a way of life. You give it up and just as quickly take it back.

Take courage, because change is tough. There are rude aftershocks. You may be surprised at your own blackness of heart. You feel like you'll always feel this way. But you won't. Somewhere along that seemingly never-ending road labeled "You'll never figure things out," you see a marker pointing onward. You tell yourself, *I won't always be in this place.* You're starting to let go.

Kari: As soon as I moved into my own house, my friend Barney, who is a child evangelist, challenged me to give beyond my normal tithe. I thought, *He doesn't understand my financial situation.* As an independent contractor, my income depended on job availability. "Okay, 35 dollars," I blurted out, figuring to myself, *What's that on top of my other losses?* In reality, Barney's challenge was about releasing fear's grip on my mind, freeing me for impossibilities: surviving a $25 checkbook balance. Restoring my relationship with Melanie. Trusting again. Remarrying.

Milestone 3: Challenge the Status Quo

You're looking through new eyes now beyond the old landscape. At first, you avoid things that make you feel bad—the bakery that made your wedding cake, the teller at the bank. You change bakeries and banks, though they're blocks out of your way.

What things make you feel good? You light candles for ambience, take bubble baths instead of showers, ask a friend to call you every day. When you examine the myths in your life, you see they can't be changed. For example, at first you believed it was good to vent your rage in outbursts. As you indulge, you see that merely pumps up the brain's arousal system. You find other ways to deal with anger: distraction, exercise, renaming the situation in a positive way. You can't change things, so you decide to change the way you think about them.

You are creating a context of success for yourself.

Noelle: When I read Isaiah's words in chapter 54, I stopped at verse 2: "Enlarge the place of your tent."

I took it literally and began to cultivate my lawn to the property line. Then I took it spiritually and acknowledged that my marriage partner betrayed himself each time he operated out of lust instead of love. And I made the most important decision of all: to affirm each evening that something larger and more beautiful would come out of my crisis. Like a self-fulfilling prophecy, my reality is being shaped by my perception of it. Not just one thing, but many things more beautiful, poignant, and even fun-filled are showing up as I allow myself to receive them.

> *Keep looking up—that's where God likes to put the rainbows.*
>
> —AUTHOR UNKNOWN

Milestone 4: Open Your Heart

You know now you will not die, though you may have wished you would. You think the world may eventually become safe again. You recognize the adventure of going to a place you've never been requires a contribution from you.

Now you focus on the woman before the wound. You wonder how to meet her again. To imagine and wonder is part of your work right now. Soon there is an intersection: one path leading to the past, the other straight ahead and up a hill. Mountains loom behind the hill, but there is no question in your mind anymore.

You put your heart into the journey.

Kari: Shortly before Ed vacated the family home, my divorced friend Eleanor offered her house as a safe place. She gave me a front-door key and cleared floor space in her hall closet where I could leave private papers. Many mornings, after dropping Melanie at school and before driving to work, I retreated to the privacy of Eleanor's living room. I needed this safe place to collect my thoughts.

But Eleanor did more than create a safe place for me. She inspired me to create safe places for myself in my own home. I splurged on a fancy bath towel with a lace-ruffled border and a coffeemaker with a programmable timer for hazelnut-scented wake-up calls. Much later, I envisioned the possibility of sitting across the table from a wonderful man who sipped coffee from a matching mug. It was then I knew: If I ever remarried, he had to love coffee (and he does!).

More importantly, I observed that Eleanor carried herself with flair. I was drawn to her enthusiasm and admired how she had put her divorce behind her despite the destabilization of her husband leaving her for a man. She was turning her hobby of oil painting into a business and had bought her own home and new dishes and had changed many things in between. She smiled a lot. "The kind of men who sneak around and walk out on marriages are not worth crying over," she said.

Milestone 5: Put One Foot in Front of the Other

It is simple. You just keep going, though you stumble now and then. You pick a wildflower while you're down. Occasionally there is a boulder in the path. You make a choice: rage at the injustice of it being there, roll it out of the way, or find a detour. You're beginning to believe in your ability to make decisions again. You are patient with your mistakes. One day at a time is good enough. That becomes your slogan. Without realizing it, you are marshaling your own feelings of enthusiasm.

With every step, you gain confidence. Your energy becomes self-motivating for all the times you are going to stub your toe. You do what you have to do.

Noelle: Early in my divorce, a young married man sat by me at dinner during at a conference and said, "I heard what you are going through. How in the world do you get up in the morning?"

Incredulous, I responded, "Three children need breakfast. Three children need to get to school. Three children need a hug to start their day." I hope he got the point. I know I did. This truth carried me through each morning, weeks of mornings, and finally years. Now the children are on their own, starting their own days, getting themselves to work. I became empowered by my own decision to rise to the occasion. I know now that one day at a time is not only good enough, but is the only way to live this fragile life.

Milestone 6: Don't Look Back

After all, "you're not going that way," it says in a book illustrated by Mary Engelbreit.[11]

However, you won't be able to count the times you'll be tempted to do so. Sometimes you forcibly pull your chin around straight, and steady your eyes with a chuckle of self-irony.

Now the possibility of real happiness is on the horizon. You are happy for the depth of character, the insight, the compassion, the change in yourself. You still haven't figured everything out, but you no longer feel you need to. Your circumstances may be imperfect, but good feelings begin to outweigh bad ones. You wear your scars like medals. You are glad you hung in there.

You are reinventing your life.

Kari: When I telephoned my parents about the possibility of a divorce, Dad said, "After a decision is made, don't look back." At first, I wrestled with Ed's decision to leave; then with my own resolution to walk on with or without him. I realized someone must have been working hard to make the marriage last 22 years; something had worked.

As the years roll on, I realize a broader application. When I'm tempted to compare myself to other divorced women on issues like joint custody and letting go of our home, I don't think, *Hey, I should have done such and such.* I look to what's ahead. Knowing I did my best with what I had at the time, I rise above regret and recrimination.

Spiritually, I now see that in a world gone wrong, it's not that God doesn't make sense. I accept that his children make choices that don't make sense. I can't do anything about that, but I know I'm part of a picture God continues to enlarge. Like Job, I've heard about the Lord all my life. Now I'm looking forward. The best is now and may be waiting in all the moments yet to be.

> *Effective people are not problem-minded; they're oppor-tunity-minded. They feed opportunities and starve problems.*
>
> —STEVEN COVEY

Look Deeper, See Further

Now you are ready to look at possibilities your heavenly Father saw before you were born. When all windows and doors to the future are barricaded, seize this golden moment. Walk to the wall and paint a window. Open it and crawl through it. The art is in knowing which reality is the illusion: the window closed in your face? or the one you paint and through which you pass to start the rest of your life? Tell yourself, *Today I will change the way I think about one thing in my life.*

"All girls are princesses," Sara said as she imagined warm muffins and soft, wooly blankets in her bare attic room, not knowing in the morning it would come true. Perhaps Frances Hodgson Burnett, author of *A Little Princess*, had been reading Isaiah: "O you afflicted one, tossed with tempest and not comforted, behold, I will lay your stones with colorful gems, and lay your foundations with sapphires. I will make your pinnacles of rubies, your gates of crystal…In righteousness you shall be established; you shall be far from oppression."[12]

The psalmist wrote, "O LORD, You have searched me and known me."[13] *Chaqar*, the Hebrew word for "searched," is a mining term. It means to probe or examine, and it carries the connotation of God digging through you deeply, as for jewels. You are of great worth.

Didn't your heavenly Father ever teach you that?

P. S.—We love you!

I Am Giving Myself a Chance

Heart Work

What can I do today to become the person I want to be tomorrow?

Chapter Eight

I Am Not Disappearing

How precious to me are your thoughts, O God!
How vast is the sum of them!
Were I to count them, they would outnumber the grains
of sand.

—PSALM 139:17-18 NIV

───

Kari: "I like what we are becoming," Richard said. My husband's shoulder nudged mine as we strolled along the Pacific shoreline. Several steps ahead, Melanie and the dogs skipped through salty surf. We had come here for lots of reasons—to soak up sunshine on this windy Thanksgiving; to let go of past memories and to make new ones.

I stuck my bare feet into the sand, digging toes into scattered clumps of broken shells. Crouching, I combed the grains for one single whole shell, but found none. A jogger whizzed by. I stood up and glanced at the trail of footprints and paw prints. In that moment I understood a truth that had eluded me before.

The Creator sees my life not as odd pieces, scattered clumps, or crushed parts of what once was whole, but as a wide, wonderful beach engraved with his own footprints. My worth is not defined by success or failure, joy or sorrow, marriage or divorce. These are just part of the picture. Divorce, by forcing me to the end of myself, was opening me to a world of possibilities much larger than myself.

That day I realized my brokenness was touching many lives with love, hope, and purpose. Finally, I saw my journey as ongoing. Life's losses are never wasted particles but an immeasurable part of who I am becoming.

> *Why else were individuals created, but that God, loving all infinitely, should love each differently?*
> —C.S. LEWIS

Noelle: One weekend I borrowed a friend's beach condo. It was stormy on the Oregon coast. One or two people braved the weather, leaving footprints in the wet sand. Most stayed behind picture windows, watching clouds move swiftly across the sky. Dressed in a hooded windbreaker, I headed north, dodging waves breaking into foam at my feet.

The beach was desolate—like my mood. Clean-swept by waves. Whipped by blustering winds. Bleak. By the time I reached the curve in the shoreline, I was soaking wet. I faced into the pelting rain, going hard after something I was unable to define, then came upon a sunken hollow in the sand about six feet wide. Every available seashell seemed to have been swept here—thousands, now crushed among pebbles and stones in the pounding surf.

I stepped into the hollow with my wet sneakers, my spirit like lead. *This is me, Lord,* I said, *Crushed. Broken. Trampled.*

Then I saw it—lying radiant as light against the gray-brown backdrop. Perfectly whole. Perfectly white. A three-inch shell, an object lesson on a vacant stretch of coastline. Promise of wholeness, purity, and what was to be. I carried it home, touched by the impossibility of its being there at all.

You Are Becoming

Perhaps you, too, have meditated to the familiar music of wind and waves and pounding surf. You prayed and carried away a meaning that is uniquely yours. As it should be. Whether you see yourself as part of a beach or a whole shell, the truth is that your worth is infinite.

"In math, if you divide an infinite number by any number, no matter how large, you still have an infinite quotient," said Charles Spurgeon, history's most widely read preacher. "So Jesus' love, being infinite, even though it is divided up for every person on earth, is still infinitely poured out on each one of us!"[1]

When your trembling toes sink deep into life's cold surf and fog engulfs you, you are not disappearing. When you think your troubles "are heavier than the sand of a thousand seashores,"[2] you are not disappearing. You are becoming. Your losses are becoming a wide, wonderful beach.

Kari: After filing for divorce, Ed procrastinated two months before moving out. Melanie stayed with him that first weekend after he moved. I awoke early Sunday morning and spent a couple hours paying bills before church. When I returned, the empty house felt like a tomb. I was so down I telephoned our associate pastor and his wife, Rod and Dot Towes, who lived two doors away. They invited me over. I could be vulnerable with them. Both had experienced an unwanted divorce. Their advice felt credible.

"Regardless of what happened, dare to dream," Rod told me. "Live with vision of what your life will be three months, six months, a year, five years from now. Have a vision for every area of your life—your job, where you'll live, new friends—what God's plan might be for the rest of your life."

Dot pulled her chair closer and looked into my eyes. "And don't overlook the fact that God is concerned with your personal life," she said. "If it's your heart's desire, have a vision of the Lord bringing into your life someday a godly husband, who will love and care for you more than you've ever been loved or cared for before—a man who will be there for you in all integrity and fidelity."

Even before I imagined a future, God was already affirming there was one. I determined to dare to dream, the way Rod suggested. I had no idea that in the morning my heart was to be further crushed. Melanie's phone conversation with "the cleaning lady" brought Ed's affairs to the surface. I felt like Job: "He breaks me down on every side, and I am gone."[3] Later that night I scribbled through my tears, "Thank you, Lord, that I can think of this as a turning point. As Rod said, give me vision. I officially mentally end my relationship with Ed. Emotionally, help me end it, too."

With hindsight, I realize that mental determination and emotional strength was not what got me through the days that followed. What helped most was learning to live with vision. Like Job, I clung to an eternal hope of seeing God.[4] But I also needed a get-through-the-day hope, like the simple faith of a child sitting on heavenly shoulders, reaching beyond circumstances, touching stars. I wanted to believe God was ordering my jobs at work and that a good man out there was looking for a woman just like me. The days I could pull this off made me feel different. Rod and Dot helped me combine a hopeful attitude (faith) with a mental picture (vision).

The next step was behaving as if I believed it.

Forget all that—it is nothing compared to what I'm going to do! For I'm going to do a brand new thing. See, I have already begun! Don't you see it?
—Isaiah 43:18-19 TLB

Your Negatives Are Developing into Positives

It takes a courageous kind of vision...

- to pop open a new calendar, thumb through months of pretty pictures, and wonder what's ahead.
- to imagine the secrets your Palm Pilot will reveal by year's end.
- to believe you'll survive the turmoil of sending your kids to their dad for summer vacation.
- to imagine Mr. Wonderful is still out there even after years of dead-end dates or lonely weekends.

Along with embracing truth, vision is another part of the hard work of healing. It is not sponge-cake faith but holy terror—shaking and believing anyway. Vision is not passive wait-and-see. It is acting as if you believe, though there are no visible or immediate results. Like letting go and forgiveness, it is a get-moving-and-watch-what-happens mentality.

Vision: You either "get it" and move on or you remain behind. You invest in your dream or declare bankruptcy. You figure there is nothing more to lose, so you do for yourself what you can do because God has a big investment in you. You are beachfront property.

Visionary people are excited, encouraged, enthusiastic. When they feel fatigued, God cooperates with their humanity. When they reach what seems like the end of the road, little miracles happen to prod them on their way again.

Elijah ran for his life from Jezebel into the wilderness, praying for death under a broom tree. God's angel did a very human thing: touched him and baked him a cake. Elijah went out in the strength of that miracle 40 days and nights; God gave him a new commission.[5]

Pregnant Hagar ran from Sarai into the wilderness. An angel found her by a spring and made her a promise that restored her vision for the child within her and gave her the will to live. Hagar called the name of the Lord *You-Are-the-God-Who-Sees.*[6]

Living with vision is a daring adventure. It is wild abandonment, releasing, loosely holding everything—including the rest of your life. It is focusing not on specific results but on a quality life in the present moment. It is daring yourself to behave as if you believe something good is going to happen, then putting yourself into a position that makes it possible to happen.

> *Imagination is the highest kite that one can fly.*
> —LAUREN BACALL

Noelle: The beach was crowded. Kids, dogs, lovers, sunbathers, sandcastle builders; and kite flyers tugged at cords that held whirling rainbows in all shapes and sizes. I'd hoped to get absorbed in the fun but was wrestling pain again—like Jacob wrestling with the angel. It was that *I-will-not-let-you-go-unless-you-bless-me* kind of wrestling. Prolonged. Lonely. Wearying. Determined.

Is there anything in my future for which it is worth hanging on tight? I wondered, remembering that four years earlier Dan and I had celebrated our sixteenth wedding anniversary on a nearby beach. In the sand, he'd written I LOVE YOU, encircled by a giant heart. Together, we'd conceived a ministry dream.

Eventually, the dream eroded like Dan's love message in the sand, pummeled by waves and scuffed away by the tread of passersby. With Dan gone, I realized the vision was as counterfeit as his wedding vows. Wrestling with the angel that day on the beach, I heard, *This is the sacrifice. Like broken water in childbirth, your broken heart, flooding your life with tears, will usher in an authentic dream.*

Though I was certain I did not want to live this vision on my own, all I could say on the beach that day was, *Lord, here I am.*

> *Write injuries in the sand, kindnesses in marble.*
> —FRENCH PROVERB

Living with Vision

"It all began with a wrong turn," writes Jack Hayford. "But for the grace of God, the story could have ended in tragedy, bitterness and death. God had something else in mind. And because He did, we have one of the most beautiful love stories ever told."[7]

Hayford elaborates on the story of Ruth, a woman of vision. He says that her husband, in moving from Israel to Moab, was looking for a new time and place, yet on his own terms. He was a man under duress seeking an answer outside the boundaries of God's provision for his people, looking for life in all the wrong places.

"Outside the boundaries of the covenant," Hayford says, "you and I will ultimately find what Elimelech, Mahlon and Chilion found—death. The untimely passing of these men is not an act of an angry God smashing a little family into the asphalt of Moab's streets. It is simply a commentary on what happens outside of the covenant…Elimelech is a man who chased a rainbow and lost an inheritance. He took his family with him and they lost everything too—including him."[8]

Hayford continues, "Before the lost could be redeemed, someone needed to retrace that costly journey and return to the place of blessing."

Retracing the journey takes vision. "Not knowing what hardships or heartaches lay ahead of her in a foreign land," Hayford concludes, "Ruth chose to cling to what was left of her new family rather than returning to the old. In so doing, she placed herself in a position to find a new time and place. The Bible says she *clung* to Naomi. She wasn't about to be turned away."[9]

Now that's vision. Ruth placed herself in a position, within the boundaries of the covenant, to find her purpose and meaning. She was unwilling to be turned away. Vision empowers because it allows you to see that your worth in this world hinges on a bigger picture—God's love for you. His love gifts you with a reality worth waiting for and hanging onto tightly.

Vision isn't about a health–wealth–happiness gospel or about channeling, psychotherapy, or autogenic training. It is about the conviction that loss equals gain, hurt can equal hope, and pain brings renewed purpose. It is knowing the God-Who-Sees and aligning your sight with his. Vision is being confident "that He who has begun a good work in you will complete it."[10]

"Therefore we do not lose heart...The inward man is being renewed day by day."[11]

So how do you start living with vision?

Kick the Devil Out of Your Hope Chest

Maybe you would like a new relationship or a different job. Perhaps it's time to sell the family home and buy a condo in another town. Or you've been approached to facilitate the church single-again group. But you're afraid. What if somebody rejects you? What if you fail?

Perhaps you know what you want and you go for it. You begin to date again, go for a promotion, or move to a new place. You get hurt. You feel defeated all over again. Maybe you volunteer to teach a class or you decide to throw a Christmas party. You fall in love, then are disappointed and disillusioned. Either way, the devil has inserted the key of fear into your hope chest and hopped in. His plan is to wear you down,[12] crush your spirit, and steal your new dream.

Living with vision, "behaving as if you believe it," kicks the devil out. You see with new eyes. Vision is magnetic and attracts like-minded people. Hope becomes a lifestyle.

Solomon offered this advice: Get on with things regardless of how the wind is blowing, because you never know what God is up to.[13] God might blow something really good your way out of nowhere when you least expect it! Get out there. Give what you've got to give.

> *One of the greatest sins a Christian can commit...is the sin of unreached potential... We allow our patterns of life to become frozen and our achievements have such low ceilings that we allow ourselves the comfort of convenience.*
> —TIM HANSEL

Place an Order for Fish and Chips to Go

Give Jesus everything in your basket right now—even if you think it doesn't amount to much.[14] After he blesses and breaks it, you'll find there's plenty to pass around.

Kari: "If there's something you feel God has called you to do and you haven't done it yet, why not?" challenged Dr. Mark Lee at a weekend family church camp tucked among the coastal redwoods.

At the time, I shuddered at the question. *My life is more uncertain than ever,* I thought. That day at camp, with our ten-year-old seated between us, Ed and I looked like any other "happy" family, but it was a mirage. In one week, our trial separation would begin.

After high school I had taken a job as a secretary to support myself through night school. Then I married Ed and worked while he got his degrees. Later I earned the family's second income. I had always put my life on hold for him.

But I'd always known I wanted to write. Childhood vacations were spent perched on riverbanks, scribbling wild and wonderful stories about pictures cut from old catalogs, while my parents fished. My grandmother insisted I tuck poems inside letters to her. Journalism teachers said, "I like the way you write."

What did God expect of me? I wondered that day at camp. I knew only too well why I had not done it, and I saw no way possible in the future. After our seven-month separation, Ed stayed for two years. Then, like the catastrophic 1989 earthquake that opened San Francisco's waterfront view by knocking down a freeway, God allowed my divorce to reveal talents hidden for two decades behind Ed's dreams. I began to see clearly and to write about what I saw. I wanted to help other people see things clearly, too.

When I remarried and was freed from the pressure of earning a second income, the stories and articles started to flow and scatter across the pages of numerous magazines. God had prepared me years before, but he was patient. When the time was right, I picked up the vision.

> *I pray that your hearts will be flooded with light so that you can see something of the future he has called you to share...I pray that you will begin to understand how incredibly great his power is to help those who believe him.*
>
> —EPHESIANS 1:18,19 TLB

Noelle: The shoreline is misty. I promised myself I wouldn't come here again in fall, but the Northwest coast is rarely clear. I drag my body through the pine trees to the beach. To think. Walking through pea soup, I pray. Imagine. Skip. Laugh.

My journey through singleness-again is taking me backward. All the way back to the five-year-old me, that little girl who wanted to dance ballet. I am reinventing that girl: independent. Proud of herself for the gifts she is exploring.

The ocean breeze is gentle, like my thoughts about myself. I am enjoying the new freedom of having young-adult children. Although I often find myself wistful for the hectic days of babies, or angry at being abandoned in midlife, good days now outnumber bad ones. I am reclaiming the woman-before-the-wound—way before.

Live Believing

Copy and tuck the following thoughts in your wallet. Read them every day for 30 days.

If I can live believing...

> *the most beautiful sunset is coming tomorrow*
>
> *the greatest meadow is the one beyond the mountain*

the closest friendship waits to be formed

the deepest love is still being created

the best answer to my prayers is already on its way

…then my life will be one of hope, expectation, and joy,

and I shall be of all people most blessed.

—Anonymous

Two people emerge arm in arm from the sandy bank behind me. They stop and embrace. They kiss. I hurt again. I want that. Part of who I am, too, is the sensual woman. As her husband grew distant and uninterested, she longed for languid nights of intimacy. I still crave what almost every woman does: a man's emotional presence, pursuit, and passion. I want to love again. *Is this an endurance test?* I ask God.

He says, *Pray for the man in the wings.* He says, *Keep becoming the kind of woman the kind of man you want would be attracted to.*

I am vulnerable, strong, weak, feminine, silly, scared, brave all at one time. I date a little. I even fall in love, but grasping at another relationship is as elusive as holding fog. How can a person ever be sure? I keep going and keep thinking about all I have to give. I wonder who the lucky man to get me will be. I'm amazed how far I have come!

If you want to leave your footprints on the sands of time, be sure you're wearing work boots.
—ITALIAN PROVERB

Look, It Is Not As You Thought

Refuse to be content with myopic vision. Life is too short to stay nearsighted or narrow-minded. Pull out your telescope. Stretch your faith. Choose to multiply God's majesty, not magnify your misery.

Vision leads past a poverty mind-set to a generosity mentality. When you see more, you give and receive more. Vision is praying for a larger map. To Joshua was given the promise, "Every place that the sole of your foot will tread upon I have given you."[15] God thinks big. He marks territory from one end of a desert to the setting of the sun and back.

"Our ideas about God are so neat and tidy, so symmetrical and right-side-up," writes Joni Eareckson Tada. "We have the Sunday School medals and threadbare Bibles to prove that we've gotten Him pretty much figured out, at least all the important stuff. Not too many things astonish us these days. But when is the last time you were surprised by the Lord?" she asks.

"Broaden your vision," Tada says. "Avoid snap judgments about His word. Focus beyond the expected. Let the Lord keep you in perpetual wonder. I have a feeling that the Lord is less interested in what we know and more interested in helping us look beyond to see the impossible."[16]

> *It is never too late to be what you might have been.*
> —GEORGE ELIOT

Jabez grew up expecting God to work; he had a vision and he went to God with it. He also had baggage; his name was a reminder of how much pain he was to his mother. "Oh, that you would bless me indeed, and enlarge my territory!" he prayed. The village bearing his name was the home of scribes.[17]

Habakkuk clung to the Lord even when his nation didn't and even though things happened he didn't understand.[18] He held on to what he couldn't see. His name comes from the verb "to embrace."

Caleb, whose name means "good," was given the land on which he set foot because he and his sons followed the Lord "fully."[19] To not follow fully is to lose much. Living with vision requires the whole heart. How often are you a mere footstep away from a promise? You, too, can be expectant. Stand on your tiptoes. Look for God's footprints on your beach.

> *One sees great things from the valley; only small things from the peak.*
>
> —G.K. Chesterton

See Things As They Are

Living with vision, you move from defining yourself as a blur or a bore who was in your ex-husband's way, to seeing yourself as God sees you. You're no longer wondering, *What will I do if I run into my ex?* You're now hoping to bump into him so he'll see how great you look. You have quit thinking, *I can't go to the big sale downtown because I might see his girlfriend.* You now imagine her expression when you look her right in the eye. You might even smile, then take yourself out for an amaretto latte! (Go ahead, admit what you're thinking. *The poor thing looks so frumpy! All that wining and dining went straight to her hips!*)

Place your circumstances beneath your feet; don't just wait for them to pass. Stride with your face into the wind, prepared for the wave of the future. "There's no stopping it," says Anne Morrow Lindbergh. Build your sandcastle with turrets and towers all over. Dig a moat that's deeper. Decorate with wave-polished stones and shiny shells. Play harder. Run farther. Fly a kite. Soar!

You see, with vision, you can hardly wait to flip open your calendar. Whatever it holds, you can face it.

> *The real voyage of discovery consists not in seeing new landscapes but in having new eyes.*
> —MARCEL PROUST

I Am Not Disappearing

Heart Work

What is my vision of how my life will be better in three months? six months? one year?

How might I be changed for the rest of my life?

Chapter Nine

It's Okay to Lighten Up
and Let Go

Cease striving [let go] and know that I am God.

—Psalm 46:10 NASB

—⟨੭⟨੭⟩—

Kari: What person standing beside the ocean's edge has not wondered about the world concealed in mystery beneath its restless surface? I did—and decided to do something about it. I learned to scuba dive. But because I get seasick on boats, I content myself with diving off the beach.

Confined inside a full-length body suit, gloves, and snorkel mask, my five-foot frame slowly trudges along the sandy beach into the rushing tide. I struggle with each step as wet sand sucks against my boots. With each forward motion, I feel the steel air tank dragging on my back, the 14-pound lead weight belt slapping my hip bones, and the foot-long instrument console swinging from the left side of my buoyancy-control vest.

The weight I carry feels unbearable as I slosh through the steel-gray swells—until I press the low-pressure air valve to inflate my vest. Soon I bob like a cork. My dangling feet tell me the sandy bottom has dropped off.

I hang for a moment suspended between two worlds. As I float into open ocean, I rinse the mask lens and breathe in the top of the regulator to make sure it's operational. Then I snap on fins, set the depth gauge, and deflate my vest; the weight I had struggled to carry now takes me down.

Below, the sun's rays skip across the edges of a coral reef. I enter a garden of creatures wiggling in unison. Purple anemones wave slender tentacles. Spotted unicorn fish nudge my arm. A white-mouth moray eel pops out of a rocky ledge, and I hyperventilate. *Stay calm,* I tell myself.

I add air to stop my descent, equalizing my weight with the water, and achieve neutral buoyancy. The jagged coral can slice my leg if I get too close. Here, I have learned to breathe through my mouth, not my nose, and to continually monitor the air pressure to ensure enough remains for my ascent. The amount of air I use and the depth of my descent determine the length of my dive.

It sounds complicated. But each time I sojourn in this weightless world, the experience is punctuated with mystery. It is ultimate solitude. The only sound I hear is my own exhaling. I can swim in any direction or somersault like a dolphin undulating with the rhythm of the sea. I am free.

> *Our light affliction, which is but for a moment, is working for us a far more exceeding and eternal weight of glory.*
> —2 CORINTHIANS 4:17

Taking the Plunge

As in diving, the weight of life's losses in divorce is forcing you to leave the surface and go deeper. If you choose to stay within safe confines under the shelter of wide umbrellas, you will miss the adventure of falling free—abandoning yourself to him who holds all things together.[1] Divorce also teaches you to breathe in a new way and to trust the only life support you need. In your own mysterious "under-see" drama, you are the protagonist coming face-to-face with your antagonist: life. Each time you dive beneath the predictable, you're apprehensive. But you are learning how to face your fears without wasting resources.

At first, your reflex is like a beginning diver drifting over an undersea ledge that suddenly plunges 20 feet. You grab hold so you won't fall. Sudden change, like the elevator effect, catches you unprepared and creates anxiety. The irony is you have achieved buoyancy; you're already floating. Now, instead of clutching people, places, and possessions for your identity and security, you are learning to let go. You fine-tune your weight between faith and doubt, glide over things you used to crash into, maintain equilibrium between too heavyhearted and too light. The more you practice, the more proficient you become.

Kari: After Ed left, I kept hearing, *Let go and I will bless you.* At the time, I didn't understand this would be one of the most difficult choices I would make, nor did I know it would be ongoing.

Early on I started releasing my grip. Things that Ed and I had possessed together no longer had meaning. Jewelry he'd given me felt tainted as I questioned his motives. I relinquished interest in his business, agreed to joint custody of our daughter, sold furniture, and gave clothing to charity.

With Ed gone, I was less distracted emotionally and had more energy to compare my rising suspicions about him with the paperwork. What I discovered pulled the bottom out from under me; but I was too late. I agonized over the decision to reopen our settlement. I wanted justice! Legal and spiritual counselors advised, *Let go.* Intuitively I sensed, *There's more here than I can handle.*

I feared Ed. I was stunned he could use the education I'd helped him get against me. However, fear of losing my health and sanity was greater. What I needed most was peace of mind. Confrontation was pointless. Battling in court might take years and keep me stuck in the past.

"In blind trust," I wrote, "I must empty-handedly dare to walk toward the future." Letting go was not a helpless resignation but a deliberate turning away from everything familiar to me—only my daily commute on the freeway stayed the same.

A couple of weeks later, Barney appeared at my door to shepherd me with this familiar verse: "...that I may apprehend that for which also I am apprehended of Christ Jesus...This one thing I do, forgetting those things which are behind, and reaching forth unto those things which are before."[2] I read it over and over. I experienced everything *apprehend(sive)* conveys: to be fearful and suspicious, to understand, to take into custody, and to forgive. It took every fiber within me to let go—of the past, of my angry desire to blast Ed about how he hurt me. Achieving neutral buoyancy in both diving and living is not easy; it takes practice. Even today, I face revelations and residue from those years. Letting go is how I cope with life's insanity as I take the plunge.

What light? I'm still looking for the tunnel!
—BARBARA JOHNSON

Weighting It Out: The Paradox of Lightening Up

Since life's currents are dragging you out to sea, you might as well go deeper. It may sound confusing, but lightening up is a prerequisite to that. It is active waiting, suspended between bifurcated worlds—the temporal and the eternal. As you prepare for both descent and ascent, you experience good and evil, joy and sorrow, light and dark, up and down.

"The ladder whose ascent implies spiritual progress has a long pedigree," writes James Hillman. "The upward idea of growth has become a biographical cliché. To be an adult is to be a grownup… [but] until the culture recognizes the legitimacy of growing down, each person in the culture struggles blindly to make sense of the darkenings and despairings that the soul requires to deepen into life."[3]

If you want your heavy experiences to take you deeper, you have to let go of surface expectations—things and emotions that keep you stuck. It is essential to lay aside what holds you back.[4] Letting go and growing down is the only way to have open hands ready to receive the life that is waiting for you. Once in the deep, weight and buoyancy become your allies.

Noelle: Weighted! My philosophy is, "You can't be too thin or too rich," but during my three pregnancies, I found that weight gain can mean value-added. I welcomed it, knowing a new possibility was growing inside me. The hard part was waiting to see what would be.

I heard that in some European languages, the word *to expect* is "to wait." "Are you pregnant?" is literally, "Are you waiting?" But these times of waiting were the most active times in my life: childbirth exercises, classes, and reading. There was time spent picking a name and preparing healthier-than-usual food, meals for the freezer, furniture for the baby's room, the layette—all the time belly and breasts getting heavier until I felt like a mythological goddess. Still, I savored every moment, knowing that the day would come when I would lighten up. I knew my "burden" would one day be born, taking on a life of her own, full of potential, expressing qualities and abilities of which I could only dream. And so it is with divorce, this new kind of burden.

If there's an experience in front of you, have it!
—AUTHOR UNKNOWN

The Way of Letting Go

Letting go is the ultimate way to say, "Your kingdom come. Your will be done."[5] Although hard to understand right now, your circumstances are, like Jonah's in the belly of the whale, an opportunity in disguise. Your fear is your limit; letting go is not for cowards. It has nothing to do with giving up and giving in. You move ahead while waiting actively for the mystery to unfold. By letting go of the happy ending to your original dream, you reposition yourself, weighted in reality. You understand more than you ever thought possible.

Letting go of the way things were sets you free. It allows your former spouse the freedom to make choices, accountable only to God, and releases you from hooks to the past. You see the enemy is a clever fisherman. He knows how to reel you back. Just as he tempted Jesus on the mountaintop with entitlements he knew Jesus deserved, he tempts you to bitterness through the empowering feelings of rage. Satan knows that if you let go, God will heal your heart and lead you closer to himself.

Letting go releases your expectations so you go even further. The failure of your marriage wasn't about you being unlovable or unloving. Maybe your ex justified his behavior by accusing you of not meeting his needs or of being lousy in bed. Maybe he loved you as much as he was capable. Letting go of your expectations for him to be courteous, generous, or affectionate allows love and him to be imperfect. You give up faulty beliefs. Your former spouse has no right to define who you are. You no longer need his approval to know what God declares: You are worthy and wonderful.

The fear of the Lord is the only true measure of a woman's worth.[6] You are responsible for simply being faithful—whatever happens. Applaud your friends celebrating anniversaries, but know that neither praying together, worshiping together, or reading Dr. Dobson guarantees love for a lifetime. Though it takes two to keep a covenant, each one of us will stand alone at the judgment.

Letting go brings you full circle: "You have hedged me behind and before, and laid your hand upon me...If I ascend into heaven, You are there; if I make my bed in hell, behold, You are there. If I take the wings of the morning, and dwell in the uttermost parts of the sea, even there Your hand shall lead me."[7] God doesn't promise to show you the future; he wants to show you himself. Are you willing to risk a descent into the deep with him...to emerge a woman who is wiser and more beautiful?

> *The future is so bright it burns my eyes.*
> —OPRAH WINFREY

The How of Letting Go

One of divorce's most crucial decisions is discerning how to let go. There are two ways to do it, both necessary at different times:

- physically letting go, getting rid of, throwing away, or carting off
- emotionally/mentally disengaging from places, people, and possessions, allowing them a different meaning

Ron Lee Davis said, "I believe you need to be challenged to take responsibility for your own feelings and to take action to assist God in his effort to make you whole."[8] Your decision about how to let go will be based upon who you know yourself to be and what is at stake. It depends on your expectations about life, whether you are an optimist or a pessimist, what you fear most, and what is most important to you.

You may know gut-wrenching fear as you confront the unknown in everything you do, from paying the electric bill or buying a house to watching your health teeter on the edge. Often things go crash, bang, bam all at once. Sometimes you don't have the luxury of mulling over what to keep, what to let go. You make decisions in a split second. Other times, the future stretches endlessly. You want to get something over with, and it gets delayed.

Letting go is inner resolve and dogged determination under stress. You want to do more than cope. Here's help:

- Put into words the choices before you. Write down pros and cons. Be specific. Keep the lists in front of you. Pray over them daily.

- Glean wisdom from many counselors. Can you tap into a church staff? A personal counselor, lawyer, or accountant who charges on a sliding scale? A friend of a friend who has gone through a similar experience?

- Remember there are risks to every choice. No one way is the right way. No one can tell you what is best for you. The responsibility lies on your shoulders. Some people want to stay as safe as possible; others risk more. There are consequences for inaction and a reaction to everything you do. Eventually you must just do it. It's okay, because "underneath are the everlasting arms."[9]

Relax! You are not responsible for everything in the universe. That's still my job.

> Love,
> God

—Barbara Johnson

Warning! Flashbacks Ahead!

It takes courage to go through a divorce. Courage is not putting up a good front, donning a happy face, thinking cheerful thoughts, and pretending "all is well." That's just fooling yourself. When a painful memory bursts upon the scene like a bigmouth eel and bares its razor-sharp teeth, stand your ground. This is a flashback. Shout back at the pain, "Only God has the right to define me. I will not give my ex or my past that power." And pray continually, "Lord, help me hold tightly to your view of me."

When Letting Go Means Keeping It Together

Legacy and family are important to you. How do you relinquish your emotional attachment to things? The day he drove away with half of the furniture, moving it to the place he (and maybe "she") would use, you were devastated. You felt cheated because those things belonged to you. It didn't matter if he had bought them before you married or they had been passed down through his family; they had been incorporated into your family—yours intertwined with his, continuous, extending into the future.

What about the things that remained with you, now tainted with memories? The antiques you purchased on your wedding anniversary? That love seat you saved so long to buy? You've looked through your wedding album so many times, cherishing how you met and the funny things that happened on that day. You'd hoped a daughter would want to wear your wedding dress, so you'd care-fully preserved it.

Through the years, you documented family life in photo albums and scrapbooks, safekeeping memories of vacations, cel-ebrations, and holidays. When he left, not only did he remove himself, but he obliterated the continuity you took pleasure in preserving. What you held precious was devalued; you can never replace it.

C.S. Lewis said, "Relying on God has to begin all over again every day as if nothing yet had been done."[10] So it is with legacy. You are what you have experienced, and that is what you pass on. Just because he is no longer in the picture doesn't mean there is no picture. You are still guardian of family history, keeper of continuity. You have another kind of legacy to give: faithfulness in adversity, grace under pressure, and the comfort of your pres-ence.

"Families come in all shapes," writes Ingrid Trobisch. "Regardless of configuration, there will always be those individuals who are the home keepers...Each of us shelter springs of our ancestral legacy, spiritual heritage and personal value which eventually flow on to those who come after."[11]

Treasure every moment. Document it. Your future comes with the fortitude to walk into it. Don't let the term "broken family" cause you to sink into despair. Sometimes letting go means holding on. As you touch the past, you come to terms with it. You assess its meaning, deciding what to keep and what to let go. You say, "These pictures are who I was and part of why I am becoming who I am now," and you resist tearing them from the pages of the scrapbook. You may choose to remove photos of him but keep his parents' wedding photo there for your children.

> *Real courage owns up to the fact that we face a terrifying task, admitting that we are appropriately frightened, identifying sources of help and strength outside and within ourselves, and then going ahead and doing what needs to be done.*
>
> —DR. ALLA RENEE BOZARTH

Noelle: When Dan moved out, I was still reeling with disbelief—while he had prepared himself for the ramifications of divorce. He warned me, "We'll have to sell the house."

"How dare you say that!" I responded. "This is my home, and the home of our children!"

Friends wondered why I would want to stay there. "Surely it must hold painful memories," they said. I saw things differently. Driven by a protective instinct like a mother bear, I determined not to lose our wonderful cottage or the peace I felt on our half acre of land.

I went to a lawyer, and then armed with legal counsel, stood fast on my decision to stay put until our youngest graduated from high school. I brought to Dan's attention that the children deserved stability through their trauma and that selling the house would force us into a cramped place where none of us would feel safe.

Dan agreed. A year later, he said he'd done so out of guilt and again insisted on selling. I stood my ground; the property settlement agreement was final.

But "holding on" to the house has meant "letting go" of emotional associations with Dan. There are reminders of his presence. Each time I rev up the lawn mower, I think of the pride he took maintaining the yard. And when I repair the pickets on the little white fence out front, I can't help remembering the summer he built it and the all-American dream it represented.

In order to move on psychologically in the place I live, I let go—not of the memories themselves—but of the pain associated with them.

Like These Ladies

You are repositioning yourself for living well, loving much, and laughing more often. You are emptying your hands to hold something new, like these ladies:

Princess Salimah lightened up. The former wife of the richest man in the world, Aga Khan (imam of the world's *Shia Ismaili* Muslims), sold $15 million worth of her jewels, including a deep-blue, 13.78-carat heart-shaped diamond.

Once a top fashion model, the princess (the former British national Sarah Crocker-Poole) told Christie's that the jewels no longer went with her new lifestyle.[12] The princess is now the ambassador for the SOS Children's Villages, an international welfare organization. She travels the world, serving the needs of needy children.

Princess Diana, from the time of her divorce until her death, was in the mode of lightening up. She dug deep into her closet and dumped her dresses. Diana placed her "working wardrobe" of fabulous gowns worn at official engagements on the auction block at Christie's in New York. The money went to charity.

Before the auction, journalist Cathy Horyn commented that Princess Diana's new look, with its "conspicuous absence of geriatric jewels and dowdy royal drapery...gives the impression that the sale of her fabled raiments represents more than closet cleaning. She is jettisoning a life that never was."[13]

> *I never hated a man enough to give him back his diamonds.*
>
> —ZSA ZSA GABOR

Less Luggage Means a Lighter Heart

The 1996 movie *The First Wives Club* was labeled by the media as a movie about revenge. But it wasn't. Although the theme involved real emotions of women dumped after long-term marriages, the movie is about what happens beyond betrayal—becoming empowered for ministry. A beautiful crisis center for women evolved out of heartbreak.

"Don't get mad. Get everything," said Ivana Trump, who played herself in the movie. For the heroines, that meant using everything they learned and received from this disastrous experience to move on and help others do the same. The first wives found a way to laugh while making their experience redemptive.

You, too, can see your heavy experience is waiting to be played with, repositioned, and reorganized. Letting go moves you into healing waters that take you beyond justice to mercy, beyond complacency to compassion, beyond what you thought would destroy you to lightheartedness.

Some days you even chuckle. He is no longer the man who has everything. Why? Because he no longer has you!

"Do you see yourself as one who is in some kind of a trial under God's training and for his timing?" asks Joni Eareckson Tada. "Let it be, let it go on, until the Lord deeply imparts in your life a rich and unique message. And then he will open doors and push you through them and let you share what you have learned for others' encouragement and his glory. You just take care to deepen your message. Leave it up to God to broaden it."[14]

Let It Go!

Purchase a helium balloon. Write a brief note about the bitterness you feel, the betrayal you didn't deserve, and the truth that can't be vindicated.

Heart Work

Tie this to its tail. Instead of stomping on the balloon, take it outside and release it. Watch it float away. It's light and buoyant. You're letting go.

Lighten Up? Here's How!

Letting go is a process. Over the coming months, you'll make decisions about what you are better off without. Cart it off, have a garage sale, or ask a friend to dump it for you.

- Get rid of the clothes you wore with him. Take a couple outfits at a time to a consignment shop and earn enough for something new.

- Sell your heavy furniture at a garage sale. Replace it with light pieces you can move easily. Or, hey, buy those five-dollar furniture-moving casters and spare Grandma's prize credenza.

- Wrap your wedding album in paper, along with love letters you've saved and any other photographs you no longer want. Shelve them upright or box them, labeled for your children.

- Get out your camera and shoot photos of your new life. Dress up for photo ops. Schedule an evening with other single friends to work on new albums.

- Sell the jewelry he bought you if it bothers you. Exchange it at the jewelers, or offer it to your daughters.

- Go through books and give away those that remind you of him. If his handwriting is in a book, but you loved it, buy a new copy.

- Take down everything hanging on the walls, freshen the paint, and rehang pictures differently. Create a new look.

- Window-shop in catalogs for new dishes or flatware. Clip pictures and glue them into a notebook. Buy one piece now and then or on a special occasion.

Chapter Ten

My Ticket Outta Here

Do not say, "I'll do to him as he has done to me; I'll pay
that man back for what he did."

—PROVERBS 24:29 NIV

———— ⟨∿⟩ ————

Of the many lakes nestled between the shoulders of Oregon's
Cascade mountain range, one is particularly serene. At 1932 feet,
Crater Lake is the deepest in the United States. This crystal-blue
body of water reflects images like a mirror. You can almost see
its bottom. But it wasn't always that way. This peaceful setting is
evidence that a fiery eruption, 42 times greater than Mount Saint
Helen's, forever changed the landscape.

Mount Mazama was once a 12,000-foot-high volcano. Pressure
released within the earth fueled a mammoth eruption. About 7700
years ago the cone collapsed in on itself. Volcanic ash covered
5000 square miles, scattering over an area that now includes eight
states and three Canadian provinces. Smoldering remains molded
a caldera, at first too hot to hold water. No stream runs in or out
of the basin; the water is replenished with yearly snowmelt. Today,

from Rim Village 1000 feet above, tourists stand in awe of the beauty of Crater Lake, looking down at eagles in flight over its surface.[1]

Divorce is also a reminder of lives changed forever. Internal pressure in the human landscape forces an eruption. Violent energy is released in the form of anger, rage, and thoughts of revenge. Hopes and dreams fail, collapsing in on each other. In the heat of it all, you can't imagine anything positive filling the gaping hole that is left.

Time goes by, and inherent in its passage is the opportunity to convert negative energy into positive, replenishing what once was with something new. Changes in your life create a hollow waiting to be filled by God, like empty hands. Now there is a way to redeem the losses. That way is forgiveness. It can transform the vacant crater into a calm setting. You clearly mirror forgiveness in a serene and transparent life.

From the hollow eyes of death, I spy life peering.
—SHAKESPEARE

What Forgiveness Is

"We can't control others, and we certainly can't force them to be good to us on our terms," says Archibald Hart in *Growing Up Divorced*. "If you have tried your best to effect healing in a relationship…but are unable to make any progress, pack your emotional bags and move on. You cannot limit your recovery because someone else refuses to go along with it…There must come a time, after we have tried everything reasonable to confront our hurt feelings, when we must claim our freedom. It is our God-given right, and our healing depends on it."[2]

But rage and hostility are automatic responses. Malcolm Boyd, an Episcopal minister and author, says the victim is ourselves when we deny our own peace, permitting anger "to burst into a hot flame inside us...Yet we are no more perfect than that hapless person locked in our past."[3] When we are able to forgive, Boyd says, our healing begins.

> *I will not permit any man to narrow and degrade my soul by making me hate him.*
> —Booker T. Washington

Forgiveness is a positive response to someone else's problem. To forgive, you do not need the cooperation of the person who wronged you, because you are saying to him, "I will not own your problem." You view your ex-spouse as human with his own set of hurts. You realize you are no longer responsible for his well-being or the resolution of his issues. You refuse to be hooked and reeled back into the relationship with its tumult of emotions.

> *Always do right—this will gratify some and astonish the rest.*
> —Mark Twain

Forgiveness is reconciliation with the past. You can never make *sense* of the past, but you can make *peace* with it and put it behind you, where it belongs. You can say, "I forgive you, but I don't have to come under your influence. I set you free from the emotional debt. You don't owe me anything. I surrender my right to take revenge." Job said, "I have not allowed my mouth to sin by asking for his life in a curse."[4] Look at it this way: Forgiveness is the sweetest revenge of all.

> *Real forgiveness means looking steadily at the sin, the sin that is left over without any excuse, after all allowances have been made, and seeing it in all its horror, dirt, meanness and malice, and nevertheless being wholly reconciled to the man who has done it.*
>   —C.S. LEWIS

Forgiveness is celebration of your new life. Forgiveness sets free energy you've used to nurture anger. When feelings become neutralized, bitterness can't harden your spirit and form a crust on your personality. Mental determination coupled with spiritual insight brings you to a place where you no longer react but instead choose your response. Old pain may erupt from time to time. Expect it. Remain receptive to God to replenish your spirit. With time, the smoldering embers die out. Long-hidden talents become visible. Dormant dreams start to grow again.

> *Many people lose their tempers merely from seeing you keep yours.*
>   —FRANK MOORE COLBY

What Forgiveness Is Not

Forgiveness doesn't mean forgetting. To forgive does not mean you pretend that the inappropriate behavior of another person never happened. It is not feigning amnesia about the hurt and saying, "Perhaps it wasn't as bad as I remember." That is rationalization or denial. Forgiveness makes conscious moral discernments in full light of the truth. You remember the injury but no longer react to the pain. It does not mean you become a milquetoast. As John Splinter explains, "Actually, forgiveness is a decision one makes because one remembers."[5]

> *Hating people is like burning down your own house to get rid of a rat.*
>
> —HARRY EMERSON FOSDICK

Forgiveness is not giving the other person power to hurt you again. A woman who has experienced physical, emotional, or verbal abuse from her former spouse may feel more in control if she does not forgive him. But unforgiveness offers false protection by setting up a boundary of resentment that is unhealthy. "For a long time, I thought my lack of forgiveness of my ex was my strength," says Ginger. "I was afraid forgiving meant I would be expected to go back to him." You can forgive without taking him back, reconciling, or (as Oprah says) inviting him home for potato salad. Unable to forgive her ex until he died following a car accident, Ginger spent years controlled by fear—and her former husband.

> *A woman who can't forgive should never have more than a nodding acquaintance with a man.*
>
> —ED HOWE

Forgiveness is not a feeling. "The one thing I haven't done is forgive Ted," says Meg, nine years divorced. "And I know I can't move on with my life until I do." Right now Meg does not feel forgiving toward the man who physically beat her, but she's determined to become willing to forgive, not for his well-being but for hers. Her willingness is the first and most important step. Like love and commitment, forgiveness is acting out of what you believe is right in spite of how you feel.

> *Our true safety lies in learning to forgive one another. Forgiveness is the most radical way of moving beyond the law of history...We can never begin anything new without forgiveness.*
> —SAM KEEN

Forgiveness is not about him, but about you. A forgiving spirit leaves you with a clean heart and open hands. Unforgiveness snuffs out the spiritual spark that propels you forward. To forgive is to obey God by giving him first priority in your life. Forgiveness says, *Lord God, you are more important than anything my ex-husband has done to me. I am willing to no longer keep score of wrongs. I need healing more than I want revenge for the hurt.*

> *It is easier to forgive an enemy than to forgive a friend.*
> —WILLIAM BLAKE

Forgiveness is never easy. Unforgiveness feeds on your fear of admitting and addressing your own bitter, critical spirit. Forgiveness is an act of the will, a declaration you won't take revenge anymore.

That doesn't mean the pain goes away. It is tough before it is tender. If this is your first attempt at forgiving, expect resistance. You are going against the grain when you decide to quit blaming another person who harmed you and when you stop wanting him to make it up to you.

> *People don't trip over mountains, they stumble on stones.*
> —OLD SAYING

Kari: After I'd settled into my house, I figured the next step was simple: Just forgive Ed—until The Neighbor shared what Ed had told her that prior Christmas: that he served me with papers and sold the house out from under me; that they needed to lie low because he had me just where he wanted me. I was ready to sign away everything, he'd said.

Did I want to forgive Ed? No. Did I feel forgiving? Of course not. Instead, I determined to step beyond my feelings with an act of my will and allow the Lord to teach me forgiveness. At first, I couldn't pray for Ed. Then I started reading aloud a paraphrase of the Lord's Prayer (see page 158), accomplishing what I could not do myself—surrendering my will. For me, the most important step I took toward forgiveness was being willing to be willing to forgive.

Today I no longer read aloud that prayer, but I still do the hard work of cleaning up my feelings when I'm attacked by Ed. For a long time, I struggled against the desire to defend myself. I battled wanting "to be right" with needing "to be whole." Control felt more about righting wrongs than turning the other cheek. It's difficult to achieve the standard Jesus set. He didn't justify himself. He didn't take revenge. He didn't accept or excuse sin. He forgave.

I don't think the process of forgiveness ever ends. Each year brings other insults and assaults—real or imagined—that force me to face personal obstacles within and without: irrational guilt over my inability to keep family together; justifiable anger over a loss of justice; a volatile mix of past hurt, present harassment, and the possibility of future hostility.

For me, forgiveness is not forgetting what happened. The photo albums from the years of our marriage are still intact. Forgiveness is not accepting or tolerating Ed's behavior; it's not changing it either. I can't. Forgiveness is what God does in me after I relinquish my right to pay Ed back with what I think he deserves.

> *No revenge is more honorable than the one not taken.*
> —SPANISH PROVERB

Noelle: "You need to forgive me," Dan said. "If you stay bitter, you'll only end up hurting yourself." That kind of patronization made the forgiveness process more complicated for me. *Did Dan think I trusted him and would accept his advice? Was he saying this just to humiliate me further? Should I forgive because it was the spiritually correct thing to do? What is real here?* I wondered.

Chris Darden, the prosecutor in the famous trial that pronounced O.J. Simpson innocent of murder, appeared on TV in front of the microphones at a press conference afterward. Darden said, "I'm not angry. I'm not bitter—" Then, starting another sentence he stopped, looked down, and walked away. Later, he admitted, "I walked away from the mike rather than lie." Like Darden, I knew that above everything I had to be true.

There was a time when anger was the only justifiable response to what had happened to me. I ripped pictures of my ex out of the scrapbooks and threw away books he had given me. But the time came to move beyond, not because of what Dan said, but in spite of it. Forgiveness became a journey that was unhurried. At first I could only pray, "Lord, Dan doesn't deserve it and I don't feel like it, but I forgive him." Each day I forgive at least 1 percent more, but I don't have to keep worrying about whether I've forgiven or not.

I told Dan, "I'm forgiving by degrees. I'm not there 100 percent, but I'm on my way." I am not giving up my moral discernment, but I am giving up my coldness toward him. With time, I'll be able to give up the stiff-arming I use to keep him at an emotional distance.

I keep offering God my spirit and asking him to keep the channel between him and me pure. Forgiveness is helping me complete the work of separation; to honor the place where my marriage hit a wall, like placing a cross at a roadside spot where someone died in an accident. Just as I continually recommitted to love in my marriage, I am continually recommitting to forgive in my divorce.

> *Always forgive your enemies—nothing annoys them so much.*
>
> —OSCAR WILDE

How to Forgive

You are standing on the ridge between Bitter and Better. This rugged divide will appear again. Forgiveness is not a one-time option. It's an ongoing choice. When a letter from your former spouse stirs up the ashes or a phone call pummels your peace of mind, it may feel like the past has a stranglehold on you. Forgiveness negates its power. It is never too late to change course and get back on track. Here's how.

Adopt an attitude of forgiving. At first, forgiveness requires that you discipline your mind and spirit. This decision is one of the most courageous you will ever make. Project yourself into the future. Decide what would make you feel as if you had dealt honorably with him. Then do that. Resolve not to retaliate, but to speak with grace about your ex-mate wherever possible. Take a mental break from anger. A vacation from hostility. A recess from rage. Gradually, you'll release the poison. With practice, you'll experience entire days or weeks of serenity. Relish them. But don't beat yourself up when anger re-ignites.

> *Forgive us our debts, as we forgive our debtors.*
> —Matthew 6:12

Be motivated by the eternal. Dare to pray for the one who hurt you. Release him to God's mercy and judgment. If you need to, use the Lord's Prayer (or a paraphrase like the one on page 158) as a pattern and read it over and over. You may have to do it mechanically at first. Accept the empowering of the Holy Spirit. "He is our engagement ring for the wedding feast of the Lamb," says pastor Dr. Larry Vold. We've been promised that the Bridegroom will return. In the meantime, the Holy Spirit acts as our guarantee and stirs up our hope. Open yourself to his comfort and his love.

Resist temptation as Jesus did on the desert mountain. Fling Satan's torments back. Put on the whole armor of God. Pray Jesus' blood over the doorposts of your mind as the Israelites painted the blood of the lamb over their thresholds during the plague in Egypt.[6]

> *Lord, if you keep in mind our sins, then who can ever get an answer to his prayers? But you forgive! What an awesome thing this is!*
> —Psalm 130:3-4 TLB

Be patient with yourself. No one says you have to accomplish forgiveness all at one time. Allow yourself to get through it by increments. Just be willing to be willing; let God keep track of the progress. Keep at the hard work of letting go and moving on, even when the fire of anger re-ignites. Just as it is easier to turn on a light than it is to drive out the darkness, give joy a chance. Let new experiences happen. Make appreciation and thanksgiving a vital part of every day. Keep wondering, *What is around the corner?*

> *The weak can never forgive. Forgiveness is the attribute of the strong.*
> —Mahatma Gandhi

Homegrown Rituals

Divorce doesn't allow for burying of the dead, because both parties go on living. There is no ritual to honor your sacred pain. Ghosts haunt those left behind and hover over future decisions: at graduations, weddings, and the birth of grandchildren. Personal rituals of forgiveness settle these emotional issues. They take skeletons from closets, put them in the ground where they belong, and bring closure.

There is no public or private ceremony to mourn the passing of a marriage. A death certificate entitled the "Final Decree" is filed at the county courthouse, but no memorial service is held when your dearly departed exits your life. Nobody brings over casseroles or stays to cry with you. There is no ceremony, no headstone, and no beautifully beribboned bouquets.

> *There is life after the death of a love.*
> —KARI WEST

Kari: Since I didn't contest my divorce, my appearance was not required in the courtroom. On legal documents, my signature, that of my ex, and the judge's verified the end of the marriage. I marked the passage alone. No one at work knew the significance of that sunny summer day; it was business as usual.

But my divorce was a death. I needed to erect a tombstone on the grave of my marriage—a memorial to acknowledge that I had belonged to somebody for 22 years. Ed received this note, prepared in advance and timed to arrive that day:

> *To the memory of a love that began one snowy Christmas;*
> *To a marriage that saw a young man's dreams of family*
>   *and college degrees come true.*
> *To a marriage that saw a beautiful baby daughter born*
>   *to a young woman who wanted nothing more than*
>   *to be a loving wife and mother.*
> *To the memory of what could have been, in sickness and*
>   *in health, for richer or poorer, "forsaking all others,*
>   *'til death do us part."*
> *May you now find whatever it is (or whoever) really makes*
>   *you happy. I do wish you well!*

Each word was carefully chosen. It was a love note to my suffering and a thank-you for what was good. It was a way to say goodbye to the me who was Ed's wife, the me who trusted him once upon a time. It was goodbye to the physical, emotional, and spiritual intimacy I thought we had once shared, to our joint history, the common ground, traditions, and goals—fulfilled and unfulfilled—we had shared. I was closing the back cover of the volume of my marriage. My feelings were an odd mix. I wanted to remember what was good. That's what forgiveness is all about.

Visit the Cemetery

If you haven't scheduled the funeral, what are you waiting for? Finish the chapter. Bury the dead. Reclaim the good, and redeem the bad. Memorialize your loss. Toss out the roses and trinkets. Kick at the dirt, if you feel like it. Wish your former spouse well. Then walk on.

In quiet moments when you are alone, thinking no one cares, remember that the most important guest at any funeral stands beside you each time you weep.

> *Mary was standing outside the tomb weeping...She turned around and saw Jesus standing there, and did not know that it was Jesus. Jesus said to her, "Woman, why are you weeping? Whom are you seeking?"*
> —JOHN 20:11,14-15 NASB

Noelle: Two years after Dan left, I spent Easter in Jerusalem on a journalistic assignment. I'd been asked to write about the resurrection and how walking in Jesus' footsteps is a new beginning every day. *Yeah, right!* I thought, remembering previous trips to Israel: the first, two years before I married, when I started praying for a man after God's heart instead of the man of my dreams. The second trip, two years before this one, when I awoke troubled one night and feeling led to pray for our marriage, spent two hours on my knees in the hotel room, believing God was at work to restore our love.

"She was weeping." The speaker's words at the Garden Tomb Easter sunrise service pulled me back to the present. "Mary was brokenhearted," he continued.

This trip, I thought, *I want to bury the vestiges of bitterness toward Dan. But how? I want God to prepare me to love again, but can I trust again?*

Than I realized Mary must have felt let down, too. Her friend, the man she'd believed to be the Son of God, the Messiah, was dead. In his darkest hour, tortured beyond recognition, he'd proclaimed words of forgiveness—despite the pain, abandonment, and rejection. Was that divinity? or stupidity? Was it love or spiritual impotence?

"Mary knew a mixture of hopeless longing and sorrow." The speaker's voice rose to my consciousness again. "She'd brought spices to lay around his body, now decaying, or so she thought. She wanted only to be with the one she loved."

Sitting in the garden that day, in the emptiness of divorce, I felt disappointed, the way Mary did finding the tomb vacant. She'd turned and looked around in the hazy dawn as someone asked, "Whom are you seeking?" But she didn't recognize the man.

Just feet from where Mary may have stood, I heard twittering in a fig tree. Two small finches swooped down and flitted playfully. Beyond them, a white half-moon faded into the pale sky. Bells from the Church of the Holy Sepulcher clanged. The finches disappeared. Above my head a blackbird took their place. It warbled a most amazing song.

"Jesus said one word: 'Mary!'"

That Easter at sunrise, it was as if he said my name, too. I was merely bringing spices to a marriage already dead. He had an encounter with resurrection in mind.

"The one who loves will always find what she is looking for," the speaker concluded.

As light fell over a garden in Jerusalem, I knew the seeds of forgiveness I'd sown would lead beyond healing.

> *If I keep a green bough in my heart, the singing bird will come.*
>
> —CHINESE PROVERB

Forever Changed

In the landscape of your life, God is creating transparent lakes out of the violent, explosive experience of loss. It appears to be the opposite of what you've hoped and prayed for. Can anything beautiful come out of so much disgrace? You doubt it. Yet under the simmering cinders, grace is his intent. You will never look at anything quite the same. With hindsight, someday you'll see his mercy in the madness, his peace in the process. For now, forgiveness is what is taking you there.

My Prayer of Forgiveness

Heart Work

When you're ready, pray this prayer whenever you need to, inserting into the blanks the name of the one who hurt you. Little by little, with willingness, this prayer, adapted by Kari from the Gospel of Matthew, will move from your head into your heart. Eventually you'll feel it and mean it. Forgiveness is your ticket out of here.

Dear _____'s Father, who art in heaven, hallowed be Thy name. Thy kingdom come and Thy will be done in _____'s life here on earth as if he were sitting beside you in heaven. Give _____ what he needs today to sustain his life. Forgive the sins _____ has committed and help _____ to forgive others. Don't test _____ beyond what he can bear. Like me, _____ is weak; please keep _____ safe from the Evil One. May _____ find peace and joy in your kingdom.

Help me forgive _____'s deception and betrayal and the pain, frustration, and disappointment he brought to me. Help me forgive _____ for the financial concerns, anxiety, sleepless nights, loneliness, confusion, humiliation, and other problems caused in my life because of his breaking covenant with you long before his infidelity to me.

Forgive me for my anger, rage, and hateful thoughts, and my part in causing our marriage to fail. Thy will be done in my life. Thy will be done in _____'s life.

Amen.

Chapter Eleven

I Am Going to Make It

I called him alone, and blessed him and increased him.

—Isaiah 51:2

In solitude, on the eastern side of the Sierras, stands the oldest living tree on earth: the 4600-year-old bristlecone pine, Methuselah. As enduring as the Egyptian pyramids, it is a testimony to toughness and resilience. Flourishing with a minimum of moisture, its roots sink into solid dolomite rock. What makes this tree survive also makes it beautiful. Gnarled and wind-twisted, its trunk grows into curved and irregular patterns, flexing with weather that includes a history of glacial ice flows. Resistant to disease, the bristlecone produces heavy amounts of pitch that ward off insects and decay.

Bristlecone pines are not sheltered in groves or forests. They grow in desolate locations at an elevation of 10,000 feet, near the timberline, where nothing else can. Stark and alone, they stand against the open sky.

> *What lies behind us and what lies before us are tiny mat-*
> *ters compared to what lies within us.*
> —RALPH WALDO EMERSON

Rooted in Ancient Rock

Too often divorce thrusts women into what feels like exile at life's remote, rugged timberline. Isolated. Cut off from the refreshment of relationships. Too much solitude. Too much history—and aging by the minute! But your roots, like those of the bristlecone, are sinking tenaciously into ancient rock.

Pat answers and clichés don't work after divorce. You must think beyond the paradigms in a way people who have not gone through it would never dare. "Americans are brought up on the fiction that there is always a happy ending—or at least, there ought to be," says psychologist Sonya Friedman. "Sitcoms, in which problems are presented and neatly solved within half an hour, hammer this message home every night. Real life, however, doesn't work that way."[1]

It's not just television and movies. There are times you would rather not go to church. It makes you feel the same way, as if all things are supposed to work out just fine if you love God. And what if they don't work out just fine? You're left alone in the church pew, wondering, *Didn't I pray enough? have enough faith? read enough scripture?*

In formerly familiar social and spiritual settings, you now feel like a round peg in a square hole. The world says, "Bloom where you're planted," or "Get a life!" The church says, "Wait on God," and "Keep your hope." But how do you handle the disorientation and isolation? You feel there's got to be more to life after divorce than continuing with the same-ol'-same-ol', heeding advice of family and friends who have never stood exposed and naked as you do. You sense they don't want to hear about it.

You're ready for a new level of faith. You know the only way is up and out in the open.

> *Stand firm in all the will of God, mature and fully assured.*
>
> —Colossians 4:12 NIV

"People who don't climb mountains tend to assume the sport is a reckless, Dionysian pursuit," says Jon Krakauer, who witnessed the deaths of three people on Mount Everest, the highest spot on Earth. "I quickly came to understand that climbing was primarily about enduring pain…It struck me that most of us were probably seeking, above all else, something like a state of grace."[2]

Krakauer's insights into this state of grace for mountain climbers are enlightening as a metaphor for divorce. Above 18,000 feet, the simple act of survival is difficult. The air is thin, brain cells die, thinking becomes confused, blood circulation slows, and movements become sluggish. Sleeping and eating are almost impossible. In the extreme cold, frostbite always threatens. Krakauer is critical of guided expeditions because they lead to a lack of personal responsibility, with the leader making all the decisions. Dependence on one person, he says, leads to lapses in judgment.

Climbing in a group does give a sense of camaraderie and support, especially in the beginning; but when push comes to shove, it is a solitary climb. Some turn back, some pass ahead of you, but whether or not you make it is solely up to your wits and stamina, and God's grace.

Beck Weathers' name was nearly added to the list of eight climbers who lost their lives on May 10, 1996—the day that saw the most fatalities ever recorded on Mount Everest. Fifteen hundred feet below the summit, when Beck's vision blurred, his guide insisted he wait to be picked up on the way back. However, the guide died further on. Eventually, Beck joined a small group descending in the plunging temperatures. But for Beck, "the lights went out." Unconscious, he was left on the mountainside, because, he explains, "I was in a hypothermic coma. Nobody comes back from that."

After Beck had been lying 15 hours on the ice, his brain began to stir. He struggled up and shuffled blindly into the wind. "I was absolutely certain I was dead," he says. Miraculously, he stumbled into camp. Astonished climbers tucked him into a shelter with a hot-water bottle. He heard them radioing back to camp referring to him as the "dead guy in the tent." But early the next morning, Beck emerged, somehow finding that state of grace that had eluded eight others.[3]

Where do you find the fortitude and resolve to get up one more time the way Beck Weathers did? How do you weather the worst to keep going?

"Everything in life offers opportunity," says Sonya Friedman, "if not always for hope, then for knowledge. Learning to accept that suffering hardship is part of life is perhaps the keystone of maturity. Coming to terms with this fact ultimately makes it possible for us to become women of substance." She continues, "It allows us to tolerate the vicissitudes of life with more resilience and understanding than we ever thought possible. It means accepting pain in our lives without inflicting it on ourselves or others."[4]

But not everyone finds this place so easily. There are casualties. One woman said, "I'm still praying for a healing so I can trust again. It's been over six years, and I'm as afraid of intimacy now as the day we separated. It's kind of frightening how protective I've become of my fragile little heart. I've been told the fortress I've built around me is so tight and strong, even the kindest, most gentle and honest gentleman couldn't begin to break through."

Like the professional guided expeditions on Mount Everest, the unaware church often leaves its own wounded to die slow, icy deaths. Bible studies on marriage are usually taught from the ideal viewpoint: the assumption that both parties are committed to life-long marriage.

There is no preparation for the possibility that one partner—even a Christian, even the one you believed God led you to—may have a hidden agenda or character defect. God does not always keep us safe. Praying together does not guarantee staying together. Too often a divorced Christian is invisible in the church, misplaced and without identity.

"Human failing is a reality of Christian experience, even among God's choicest men and women," says Dwight Small. "But God's grace is redemptive and restorative. So we adhere to the divinely ordained norm for marriage with full commitment, and we hold high the ideal. But if the ideal is missed and a failed marriage results, then we, as responsible ministers of God, must help broken and hurting individuals find the best possibilities in God's abundant provision."[5]

Kari: "You are born alone, you live alone, and you die alone," my mother always said. I never understood her words until Ed left. I had deluded myself that *being* the right person, as my child-hood Sunday school teacher had said, was more important than *finding* the right person. Trying to be a Proverbs 31 woman, I'd looked after my household, earned a living, and even worked with my hands—sewing drapes, making my clothes and Melanie's, raising vegetables, making jam, winning blue ribbons at the county fair for my knitting and crochet work.

But my love, integrity, effort, and faith could not keep my marriage together. I had depended upon another human being to always be there, when he may not have been capable of lifelong commitment. Nothing had prepared me for that possibility.

Several years ago I discovered how repulsive that seven-letter D-word is in the Christian community.

When I appeared on a Christian radio broadcast with two other women, there was negative response from several listeners decrying the fact that the program hosted two divorced women.[6] "That's just the point," we said. "We are evidence that divorce cannot be avoided sometimes, regardless of how much we wish it could."

Don't people get it? we wondered.

The Divorce Dilemma

After interviewing a random selection of adults nationwide, half of whom were born-again Christians, the Barna Research Group (in the premiere issue of their newsletter) found that "born-again" adults were slightly more likely to go through a divorce (27 percent vs. 23 percent of non-Christians). Those who described themselves as Christian fundamentalists were even more likely to get divorced (30 percent). With data like this, Barna concluded that the Christian community must re-examine the ways in which family matters are addressed within church ministries.[7] Solving the divorce dilemma is one of the urgent, critical issues facing today's church. Not only should we address how to prevent it, but what to do with adults devastated by it and children growing up in divorced families.

> *Divorce takes its toll; please have exact change.*
> —NOELLE QUINN

Noelle: One evening in church, the pastor asked the congregation to pray for people sitting at home who might be considering suicide. I thought, *Why not admit there is pain within the church, not just outside it? There are people sitting in this very congregation right now in so much pain they have thought of suicide.* I was one of them, but I didn't say a word because everybody still had their Sunday masks on, including me.

Months later, the pastor asked the congregation to name what they were grateful for. The first woman to speak said, "God healed my marriage." Everyone cheered, "Hallelujah! Praise God!" Since by that time I'd accepted the truth about my former spouse and was thankful to have moved beyond the relationship's toxic parameters, I felt like raising my hand and saying, "God delivered me from my marriage." I wonder: Would the congregation have cheered? Would the pastor have kept his smile?

> *A fool sees not the same tree that a wise man sees.*
> —WILLIAM BLAKE

Life in Exile

Sociologists have studied the reaction of the church to divorce. Dr. Ray DeVries says, "The Church simply does not know what to do with you [divorced people]. You are walking manifestations of our uncertainty." DeVries explains that traditional religions have difficulty facing the modern world because modernity changes religion, even the safe world of evangelicalism. "We are becoming more secular in that we are increasingly rational, private and civil, leaving us confused about our identity."

DeVries says the church is asking, "We are called apart from the world, so how can we accept you? If we accept you, won't others be encouraged to get divorced?" He claims people who are divorced bear the brunt of evangelicals' ambivalence about accommodating the modern world. "We're not sure how much accommodation is too much. We constantly juggle the doctrines of creation, the fall and redemption. But we have a tendency to focus on the fall. We become legalistic because the human response to the fall is to construct careful codes to live by."

"The doctrine of redemption offers a different message," DeVries declares. "If we focus on redemption, we emphasize grace. Perhaps divorce needs to be seen as a manifestation of God's grace rather than a violation of our legalism."[8]*

If you have children, you know too well that divorce has residual effects the church has yet to address. Statistician George Barna found "that within two years after divorce, most single parents abandon the Christian church because they sense condemnation and rejection." The effect divorce has on the generations that are paying for the sins of their fathers, Barna says, "is not a pretty picture."[9]

"The effect of the parents' divorce is played and replayed throughout the first three decades of the children's lives," says Judith Wallerstein, who studied 130 children from 60 marriages for 25 years. "We selected well-educated, middle-to-upper class parents for the study," she says, "because we wanted to see divorce under the best of circumstances." Wallerstein's findings, presented at the second World Congress on Family Law and the Right of Children

---

* If you would like to learn more about the theological viewpoints on divorce, remarriage, or both, read *Divorce and Remarriage: Four Christian Views*, H. Walter House, ed. (Downers Grove, IL: InterVarsity Press, 1990).

and Youth in San Francisco in 1997, revealed an adult's experience reaches a peak at breakup and levels off, but the effects of divorce on children are cumulative and increase over time.[10]

Noelle: My firstborn child displayed great resilience and diplomacy with both parents as we navigated divorce. She was my strength and, I also think, her father's. I was grateful for the maturity she exemplified to me and in front of her sisters.

Then one night she broke down at my bedside and cried. "Now I'm always going to be afraid Todd [her long-term boyfriend] will leave me," she said. My spirit sank. I knew that, but I had never expected her to articulate what Wallerstein writes about. "Children of divorce feel the lack of a template for a loving, enduring and moral relationship between a man and a woman," Wallerstein says. "As their anxieties peak throughout society, the full legacy of the past twenty years will begin to hit home."[11]

> *Forgive us for turning our churches into private clubs…*
> *for pasting stained glass on our eyes and ears to shut out*
> *the cry of the hungry and the hurt of the world.*
>   —A 1968 LITANY FOR HOLY COMMUNION,
>   UNITED PRESBYTERIAN CHURCH

Kari: Nobody knew the obstacles I faced getting Melanie to go to church in the first place. I had to overcome her dad's negative innuendos on top of normal teenage resistance. All I had asked was that she show up once a week until she graduated from high school. It was her choice whether she chose church, Sunday school, or Wednesday-night youth group. She went willingly—until a particular Sunday-school discussion turned critical of divorce.

Embarrassed, Melanie admitted her parents were divorced. "Wasn't 22 years enough?" she sobbed.

Later she snarled at me, "See if I ever go back to church again." I'm both grieved and outraged at the insensitivity of the family of God—until I recall my former "I'll never be divorced" attitude.

> *We must not make assumptions about God's love based on the way people love.*
>
> —DR. PAUL MEIER

Take It to Heart

Perhaps these letters to a women's magazine may encourage you to grace fellow climbers:

- "Thank you for reaffirming the truth that there is struggle in the Christian walk. I long to know the One who is 'not afraid to touch your hurts.' I have so many! I have become numb from hoping someday God will remember me, too. Cynical? A little. Bitter? Somewhat. Real? Absolutely. But this is where I am and if I am ever going to meet my God, it will be right here. Where it hurts."[12]

- "When I feel overwhelmed, I read the article [about divorce] again....It gives me comfort and strength. Thank you for printing a wonderfully insightful and brutally honest real-life story."[13]

- "[In] the article...you spoke that ugly word—divorce—out into the light. It didn't contaminate, but helped me see that I still can be a woman of virtue."[14]

That is where you are right now—a woman of virtue, human and divine. God calls you, an out-in-the-open struggler built for the climb, to reality living. Tap into your resources. Get gritty. Meet life with wind in your hair. Tell the truth. Reality is not about rigidity but about being grounded in your faith, taking life as it comes. You ordered mercy, but God delivered grace. You are not a delicate hothouse plant tucked under a porch. Now you are enduring the cold. You know living fully is not about rescue but resolve. Jesus has overcome death, divorce, and whatever else you face.

> *Empathy is the human reflection of the incarnation...*
> *We possess the ability to enter the pain and joy of others.*
> —Dr. Dan Allender

Gnarls Mark the Storms

Stability is not about where you live, who you're with, or what you own. Stability lies within you—an invisibly rooted mental fortitude and emotional well-being that draws nourishment from the Rock of Ages.

"As we get older...we come to love the gnarls that mark the storms that have been weathered and the scars that give silent testimony to suffering born with dignity," writes Sam Keen. "The presence of evil may break the heart, but it does not prove the cosmos is a loveless place. To the contrary, sacrilege helps us locate the sacred because when confronted by torture or desecration, we know life should not be violated."[15]

The paradox and the power is that endurance and perseverance turn loneliness and fear upside down. Endurance and perseverance are "qualities we would all like to possess," says Jerry Bridges, "but we are loath to go through the process that produces them." Bridges says *endurance* is the ability to stand under adversity; *perseverance*, the ability to progress in spite of it.[16] These qualities enable you to become a woman of substance. Being alone again carves a unique groove of approachability. You have been there! You know how *alone* feels.

Next time you meet an elegant lady standing alone on the timberline, let your echo carry far. Shout, "Hey, there's a great lover if I ever saw one. She stands with grace. She's living fully and loving well. She's making it." Then tell the world, "Guess what—I'm going to make it, too!"

> *They are so weak that the wind can carry them off! A breath can puff them away. But [she] who trusts in me shall possess the land and inherit my Holy Mountain.*
> —Isaiah 57:13 TLB

P.S.—You *are going to make it!*

I Am Going to Make It!   Heart Work

I am seeking a state of grace. I realize that in this experience lies opportunity. I will embrace my pain and keep going. Today I will write an affirmation about myself and place it where I can read it first thing every morning.

Chapter Twelve

It's Time to Thrive

Love...bears all things, believes all things, hopes all things, endures all things. Love never fails.

—1 Corinthians 13:4,7-8

Noelle: Early one morning on a summer vacation with my daughters, I went beachcombing. Along the Pacific shore I saw a sign that said this: "Life in the Crash Zone: Wind against sea creates friction, causing waves to crest, then break with fury against the shore. Anything that finds itself in this crash zone has to hide out or hang on for dear life."

No one could have better described my life. I thought of Cynthia in the movie *First Wives Club*, who jumped over a penthouse balcony after her husband walked out. If I had not hung on for dear life, might I have crashed the way she did?

I hoped my future would unfold as blossom petals do in those high-speed science films. I'd been through the hibernation and the crazy get-out-and-go-girl stages. I'd prayed my heart out. I'd journaled my brains out. A whole shelf of dog-eared notebooks under my bed was testimony to that.

Encouragement came in smatterings. Like Cynthia, I got over my ex but found loneliness the long-term killer. What was I supposed to do when my teenagers split in all directions? My best friend was dating, my married friends stayed home, the Christian singles group was flaky, and local nightspots were just places I'd meet people like my ex and The Neighbor. A family member, tired of my complaints, communicated, "Move away or shut up about it." That didn't help my loneliness a lot, either.

At the beach, I was thinking about the uncertainty that could put me over the edge; then I read the last phrase on the sign: "Yet a multitude of fragile life thrives right here in the crash zone." Thrive? I'd hoped just to survive. That day I decided to dig my toes deep into the foamy sand of the beach I'd been cast upon: I would refuse to fade away. I vowed not to disappear or crack up. I was determined not only to endure, but to flourish, succeed, shine.

Look at your feet. You are standing in the sky.
—DIANE ACKERMAN

Surf the Stops, Starts, and Surprises

Thriving after divorce is surging forward, tugging backward. You are alive and breathing in a restless, shifting sea. Like coral reefs enduring a pounding environment, you have to will to thrive.

You'll find that nothing on this earth can propel you toward the future and away from a toxic past faster than enthusiasm. It will cause you to stabilize right where you are and then go somewhere different. If you keep doing things the way you've always done them, you'll never have more than you've always had, or be more than you've always been. If you want to change your life, you've got to build on changes within yourself. The pivotal point is the quality and degree of your ardent fervor for life.

"How can I," you ask, "after what happened to me?"

It's not difficult. You decide when you want to feel enthusiastic. You decide how impassioned you want to feel. You decide and you determine just how dramatically you will let exuberance change your patterns of behavior, your outlook on circumstances, and your charge into the future. Will you open your arms and become infatuated with life—or keep them clutched over your breast, withdrawn and afraid? Today you can make one change. You may as well, for the past is no longer an option.

"Let's face it," says Dory Hollander, "when you've traveled a path strewn with evasive deceptions, lies of exclusivity, broken promises, and a deliberate avoidance of straight and honest talk, it really is time for a change....However, changing partners won't be enough. If you're sick of what you've been putting up with, you have to consider changing the only person you can change—yourself."[1]

If you adapted to him all those years, now do it for you. Adaptation in the name of love is part of a woman's repertoire from the beginning. You are brought up to respond and surrender: time, energy, affection, your body in lovemaking. You anticipate needs and respond to them, promising you'll be there.

You pay an enormous price for this 24-hours-on-call availability. Your boundaries are blurred by overlapping responsibilities. On the job you wonder about your child at day care and plan dinner in your mind. At home, you iron both your clothes and the family's, catch up on paperwork, make dentist appointments. Your personal fuel tank often runs on empty. When you think back, can you recall your former spouse pressing your blouse or dicing veggies for the

Crock-Pot before he left for work? (If so, please write us; we want to know your secret.)

You had geared up to continue to adapt for what was supposed to happen at this time of life, but wildly divergent changes were forced upon you. Now is the time to respond to the hunger of your own soul.

A [wo]man is not old until regrets take the place of dreams.
—JOHN BARRYMORE

Kari: My garden thrives not because it's in a tropical zone or on a level piece of ground—it's in neither of these places. It exists because it tolerates extremes: scorching sunlight, mildew-generating fog, an irrigation well that often runs dry, and hungry gophers chomping at roots.

"I'm amazed how that hill has responded to your touch—your faith was great," my mother told me, describing the steep, arid California hillside I turned into a lush habitat. It shelters not only fruit, flowers, and vegetables, but wildlife. A variety of birds, butterflies, raccoons, skunks, foxes, and reptiles find sanctuary there.

Mother is right. Tackling slopes, stubborn clay, and hilltop winds takes gutsy faith—both in my garden and my life. It is hard to believe that the thriving woman I am today once journaled, "God, there isn't enough strength anymore to hang onto your promises. I'm on the brink, ready to crack up." Often I thought I had wasted the best years of my life on Ed.

But it isn't true. Thriving isn't about an ideal location, perfect timing, or climate control. It's happening now as I endure opposition and refuse to give up—whatever I face. As much as I want my life to be a tropical vacation, friction is here to stay. When the gopher turns my flower beds into a war zone, either I slam the gate never to return, or I figure he was there first. I endure his rototilling because it makes my digging easier, aerates the packed soil, and unearths surprises, like castoff pieces of flagstone fit for a footpath.

Sure, I rail at life's unfairness. What rubs against me creates heat. But more often than not, friction's heat drives my resolve to sling open life's gate and brave the elements one more time. Besides, I don't want to miss a great garden and life that's on the grow.

Exceeding Abundantly Beyond

Surprise yourself. Say *yes* to opportunities instead of thinking, *Oh, I couldn't do that!* Come up with one or two snappy aspirations, and trust El Shaddai to bring along the means and ways if he wills it. Dare to believe he does. Unless you have evidence to the contrary, believe that your burning desire was placed there by him. Look as far into the future as you dare, for it is all yours. Within the possibilities of faith are all you long to be and all you long to do.

Practice boomerang joy. "Boomerang joy" is something author Barbara Johnson loves to talk about. Sharing boomerang joy means you'll be more playful, give more compliments, and conceive at least one idea a day to cheer someone else. You learn to do random acts of kindness with panache. And the joy comes tumbling back. You don't look for results and it doesn't always come from the same source, but what you give away is never wasted.

Maintain a professional distance from the devil. As you decide to be enthusiastic and go for God's gusto, that's exactly when Satan is going to show up and try every trick in the book to pop your balloon, rain on your parade, and take away your sugar bread.

Be like Martin Luther, who woke up one night in fright, opened his eyes, and saw the devil standing at the end of his bed: "Oh, it's only you," he said calmly as he turned over and went back to sleep. Don't let fear attach you to the devil.

Make the most of the fact that well-being attracts. When asked to list what attracted or repelled him as a single man meeting women, Kari's husband, Richard, said he wasn't attracted to women who were preoccupied with their own healing, exhibited a "poor me" attitude, or made gender-specific comments like "all men are jerks" (even in joking). Those he liked and wanted to know better were women who showed a positive attitude and were outgoing, curious, stimulated by new ideas, and able to converse on a variety of topics. Your vitality is a magnet for friends and opportunities.

> *It's kind of fun to do the impossible.*
> —WALT DISNEY

Noelle: At a darling spoof on Pity Parties I attended, a woman who had also been dumped said she'd given up being concerned what her body looked like. "Who cares anyway?" she said. I was flabbergasted and thought, *How could she not care?* Being healthy and fit is more important to me than ever. I drink a lot of water to hydrate my skin and brain, and I exercise aerobically three to four times a week. Feeling good creates momentum to look good, and looking good motivates me to be more outgoing and friendly.

But all the makeup in the world doesn't substitute for lack of twinkle. That's why I stimulate hope however I can: combing bookstores for inspirational writing, seeking out people who've got pizzazz, listening to Mozart and Tina Turner, playing with puppies and polliwogs.

Still, I want more ways to thrive. I've always been conservative, thrifty, economical. "Make do" was my motto. One day I decided, *Enough of that!* I'm changing my poverty mentality and becoming generous, even to myself. I practice giving for sheer pleasure, indulge myself, and embrace the eccentric, the bizarre, and other people's quirks—everything that's wild as long as it is wonderful, too. I am emerging. I'm changing from within while learning to be at peace with what I can't control.

> *Age may wrinkle the face, but lack of enthusiasm wrinkles the soul.*
> —AUTHOR UNKNOWN

Kari: I found the ability to adapt and grow goes far beyond those "be content whatever the circumstances" sermons. I recall the panic and confinement I felt in the beginning as I adjusted to being single-again in an unfamiliar house. Little sun came through the windows. And it wasn't the lack of activity that got me down. After a full day's work, I came home to more: sorting laundry as my printer pounded out the work I had brought home; helping with homework as I proofread. I appreciated friends who helped me regain my sense of self and showed it was possible to make a new start.

I thought of my mother's garden, created with "starts" from friends and relatives. My great-great-grandmother tucked a wild yellow rose root in her trunk when she emigrated from Ireland. My mother passed one on to me. "Nurturing a new start takes my mind off myself," she says. "I think about where it came from."

Each time a start is given away, it will need to adapt to a new environment, and it does better if given extra attention.

Friends who were transparent helped me confront my fears; I saw how they had grown through their losses. They helped me accept the divorce card I had been dealt by showing they held different ones that weren't necessarily better: widowhood, illness, problems with children. They gave me confidence that I, too, could adapt and thrive on my own again.

Nurturing also came from those who didn't know what to say but stayed in touch anyway. "I apologize," Mary said recently. She and her husband had been our next-door neighbors for more than ten years. "I had no idea what you were going through or I would have done things differently." Yet I treasured her telephone calls, invites to tea, and help taping my new answering-machine messages. Just remaining my friend was enough.

Arlene had to pursue me. My friend since grade school, she'd been my maid of honor. Embarrassed by the divorce, I seldom stayed in touch, and she couldn't come to my wedding when I married Richard. When we met again later, she shared her own troubles. We cried together. I popped open a dusty box of journals and for the first time shared them with another person. Arlene gave me permission to touch my pain again and see it from a distance. The high and low moments I had endured in my crash zone helped her cope with struggles in her marriage.

He comes alongside us when we go through hard times, and before you know it, he brings us alongside someone else who is going through hard times so that we can be there for that person just as God was there for us.
—2 CORINTHIANS 1:3-4 MSG

Symbols That Life Goes On

Friends boost your immune system, according to public-health psychologist Blair Justice. A landmark study at the University of Michigan revealed that "the lack of supportive relationships is a factor that is almost as dangerous as well-known risks such as smoking, high blood pressure, or obesity."[2] True friends sense the velocity of the wind against your soul, knowing when to encourage or simply say nothing. When your hopes are dashed, friends encourage you to keep your chin up. With true friends, you do more than survive circumstances; you surmount them. You believe you can start again. Here's what some divorcing women did:

Debbie refused to withdraw. She found a friend to share secrets with—Robbie, who pulled her into the singles group. They started a singles pew in their church.

Jane was afraid nobody would like her if they knew her struggles. After she joined a parents' committee at school, she met Jack and Sharon, who included her in weekend outings.

Carrie invited an elderly friend for donuts and a visit to a garden nursery every other Saturday morning. She says, "The companionship and mutual interest in flowers took away the loneliness."

Katherine didn't have children, but she knew that healthy touch heals. She put her name on the calendar: a haircut every five weeks, a facial, manicure, a massage now and then.

When Karen's brother-in-law, Allan, said, "You troubled the marriage so he had to go outside to meet his needs," she started defending herself. Then, realizing Allan had shame issues similar to her ex's, she let it go. When he later accused, "You have never admitted your responsibility," she responded, "I realize I forced him out because I wouldn't accept his mistress—and failed to meet his needs for large breasts. Do you get it, Allan?"

Barb's best friend never wanted to marry again; but Barb didn't feel that way. She chose to believe the longings of her heart validated God's will for her. She realized no Mr. Wonderful was going to make everything perfect, but she kept handing her feelings to God and claiming his promises.

June called Linda after every harassing phone call from her ex. Linda was smart enough to say, "I love you. You're going to be all right," every time.

Beth's formerly close friends shut her out but invited her ex and children over for social occasions. Instead of starting a feud, she realized friends like that were not a big loss and found moral support elsewhere.

Kate had always longed for sexy encounters with her husband, which never happened; now she wanted a handsome man to come along and rip her clothes off. When Monica told her, "Yeah, what you need is to get laid," Kate thought about it; then her own values won out. She knew she had to live with herself.

Kari visited Israel when Melanie spent the first Christmas with her dad. That summer, she met her parents for trout fishing in Colorado during the week her daughter spent at camp: "I needed something to look forward to and needed interaction with others."

Noelle felt like staying in after the news of Dan and The Neighbor broke in their small town, but she forced herself out to community and school events. "My children's welfare took priority over anybody's perception of what had happened. Besides, I ended up having a lot of fun with the people around me."

The essence of genius lies in knowing what to overlook.
—WILLIAM JAMES

Wiser in Love

Kari: I was carrying a pot of baked beans to a barbecue when I met the man of my dreams. It was an ordinary day. In the months that followed, I danced between afraid-to-trust-again and wanting-to-risk-it. I told the Lord to take this man out of my life if he wasn't right for me.

Shortly before Richard asked me to marry him, he learned of an acoustic neuroma (tumor) behind his left ear. Without surgery his life expectancy was only two years maximum. Since surgery might leave his face paralyzed, he thought it best to end our romantic involvement.

"If that's what you want," I said as he turned to walk to his car.

Richard turned around. "I know what I want," he said, "and I'm looking at it." The crisis solidified our love. Together, we determined to cope with whatever happened. I addressed wedding invitations in the hospital waiting room while he underwent the risky eight-hour operation. The surgery left him with balance and hearing on the right side only, and an unexplainable nerve-related ringing in the deaf ear. In addition to tolerating this constant internal noise, Richard had to learn to walk, drive, and ride a bicycle all over again.

The two of us held few illusions about riding off into an exquisite sunset. I'm glad, because four days before the wedding the Loma Prieta earthquake shook the area. Shipments into San Francisco were curtailed, including deliveries of cut flowers. When the lady creating my bouquets shared her dilemma, I said, "Then we'll get a chrysanthemum plant at Safeway and whack off the flowers." When the windows fell out of the hotel we'd booked for our wedding night, we settled for any available hotel room.

Several guests called to say damages would prevent their atten-
dance; we went on with the ceremony.

For me, thriving is picking yourself back up and going on with
the ceremony of living. The only time I won't be hanging on for
dear life is when I'm dead. Although finding a second love is an
enviable position to be in, I know that having a life partner isn't
a shield from crash zones.

> *The best things are the nearest; breath in your nostrils,*
> *light in your eyes, flowers at your feet, duties at your hand,*
> *the path of God just before you.*
> —ROBERT LOUIS STEVENSON

Noelle: "How do you do this single stuff?" I asked a never-
married friend. "I'm not getting the hang of it."

"Now you know why I'm so neurotic!" she replied.

I laughed. In spite of what I'm missing, some days I know I'm
happier than I've been in years. Statistics show men get married
faster after divorce, whereas women tend to adapt better, appre-
ciating the autonomy singleness offers. Even when they didn't want
divorce, a whopping 80 percent of women say they are better off
afterward.

I have to admit, part of my joy comes in the potential of meeting
a man who also wants to commit to romantic love. I've heard remarried women say, "Now I know how love is supposed to feel."
Actress Jane Seymour said on an *Oprah* broadcast, "I came out of
a very bad situation and didn't know if I would ever know love
again. When I did, I realized it was the only love I'd ever known."

Something about these statements touches me. I hope to be
wiser in love; I know I am in life. My days may be uneventful,

but they're filled with more than romantic dreams. My inner life is rich. Besides, there are kids to raise, flocks to feed, wounds to tend, people to bless—the "I've been there" kind of blessing only I can give. And I think that I'm about to!

> *The vision is yet for an appointed time; but at the end it will speak, and it will not lie. Though it tarries, wait for it; because it will surely come.*
> —HABAKKUK 2:3

Surf's Up

Life in the crash zone is wind-whipped and scary. But each surging breaker is like the contractions of childbirth. With each pulse, new life is pushed farther onto the shore, like intricate driftwood and beautiful shells in which a multitude of fragile living organisms thrive. Hidden in the crevices is a multitude of microlife that has adapted to the rush, the roar, and the rhythm. You, too, can live in the crash zone. Though pounded, you won't be crushed. Knocked down, you'll get up. Let enthusiasm and exuberance drive you forward.

It's Time to Thrive!

Using indelible ink, write your name on a seashell or a small rock. As you place it on your nightstand or desk, remember that persistence pays. Soon you'll start to thrive!

Heart Work

Chapter Thirteen

I Like the New Me

We speak the wisdom of God in a mystery, the hidden wisdom which God ordained.

—1 Corinthians 2:7

⁓᧕᧒⁓

All she had to do was enjoy life: a $20-million fortune, a thousand dollars a day in royalties. But Sarah could not. This 44-year-old widow was afraid of the dead.

Following the death of her husband, William Wirt Winchester (the rifle king's son), in Hartford, Connecticut, Sarah consulted a spirit medium in Boston. Séances confirmed her fears—the Winchester Rifle fortune was haunted by the ghosts of millions of Indians, settlers, and animals killed by the "repeater" rifles that won the West! Messages from the spirit world insisted that Sarah make her surroundings appeal to first-class spooks who would confuse and keep the evil ones away. "Get a larger house," the spiritist advised. "Fix it up however the spirits require."

So Sarah Pardee Winchester crossed the Continental Divide and bought an 18-room house on six acres south of San Francisco. For the next 38 years, carpenters worked 24 hours a day as she pored over building books. Sitting in the séance room at the heart of her house, Sarah devised bizarre plans for remodeling and enlarging what is now known as the Winchester Mystery House in San Jose, California. She did not live to build but incessantly built to live.

The puzzled workers did not know that the Boston medium had promised nothing bad would happen to Sarah as long as hammers rang. Workers were hired and fired. "Build switchback stairs here; two-inch risers there," they were told. "Tear down that column; rebuild it upside down." The house became a 160-room mansion overlooking lavish gardens and a view of the Santa Clara Valley beyond. The mansion had 46 fireplaces, 13 bathrooms, 3 elevators, rooms with rare scalloped French Lincresta wall coverings. It rose seven stories, until the 1906 earthquake reduced its highest point to a fourth-floor balcony. Whatever the spirits wanted, the spirits got, including a priceless Tiffany window installed on an inside wall where daylight never reveals the multicolored radiance for which it was created.

The hallway to the center of the home is like a maze. A stairway leads to a wall with no door. Several doors open to solid walls. Lighting is arranged so no shadows are cast. Windows have 13 panes; walls, 13 panels; chandeliers, 13 globes; and the greenhouse, 13 cupolas. At Sarah's request a bell tolled at midnight, 1 A.M., and 2 A.M., as a signal for spirits to scurry back to their graves.

Mrs. Winchester refused to be photographed. Only her Chinese butler was permitted to see her face. After an earthquake trapped her in a front bedroom, Sarah sealed off that part of the house, allowing no one entrance through the front door, including then-President Teddy Roosevelt.

At her death in 1922, only four million dollars remained of the fortune. Her rambling home remains unfinished, a brooding reminder of a reclusive, fear-driven woman. Although she lived in a richly furnished house full of French beveled-glass mirrors, 52 skylights, and more than 10,000 windows, Sarah Pardee Winchester was controlled by darkness.[1]

> *The worst evil of all is to leave the ranks of the living before one dies.*
>
> —SENECA

A Fabulous Fortune

Divorce vests you with a legacy of destruction, but inherent in that legacy is the opportunity to acquire holy wisdom. With your divorce, you crossed a dividing line. You'll never live the way you did before. Wisdom shatters illusions, opens doors, dispels darkness by letting in light. You need no longer hunker down, wounded, silent, walled away in a warped reality. You are not a frumpy farmhouse; God intends you to be a richly furnished mansion.

Your eternal spirit houses awesome things prepared by a loving God, whose Spirit is leading you into all truth. You now touch the hidden things, but not through magic or a medium.

Under the leadership of Jesus, you are illuminated and enlightened as you traverse the *mase* of divorce. The use of the word *mase* dates back to Chaucer in the 1300s. It represents, in the face of many obstacles like deception, delusion, and disappointment, a journey to seek the center of truth.

> *You thought you were going to be made into a decent little cottage? He is building a palace. And he intends to come and live in it himself.*
>
> —C.S. LEWIS

Inherent in divorce is an opportunity to possess the priceless wisdom of discernment (a clear mind) and insight (the ability to see with your spirit). Priceless wisdom makes you savvy. An internal light bulb clicks on, allowing you to see more than you saw before.[2] What you discover is not what you expect—you can now put your finger on subtle discrepancies. You can begin to identify irrational thinking as it occurs, and you can confront it. You can begin to see through manipulation and the emotional control that may have been used against you in the past. You connect with your own integrity.

Ingredients of Integrity

- *Discernment:* to perceive by the sight or other sense or by the intellect; to distinguish mentally.
- *Insight:* an instance of apprehending the true nature of a thing through intuitive understanding.

"O LORD, who may abide in Your tent?" asked the psalmist.[3] The answer: "He who walks with integrity, and works righteousness, and speaks truth in his heart." Integrity is the sum of the equation when you combine discernment with insight. Webster's defines *integrity* as "uncompromising adherence to moral and ethical principles, soundness of moral character; honesty; the state of being whole or entire."

God's desire for you is this state of being whole, the reintegration (or integrity) of your soul, spirit, and body after its fragmentation in divorce. His principles work. You are wise to rely on what you know is true and on the one you know is the truth.[4]

As your integrity is confirmed, your femininity is affirmed. It shows in the way you carry yourself. Walking through the maze, and sticking with your aspiration for a better life, you can acquire an air of reverence and grace that makes you charming and interesting. What you are going through will add to your mystique. You wear strength and dignity well.[5] People are attracted by what you stand for: innocence, purity, and a tender heart. As you follow God, ingest his Word, and refuse to be sidetracked by pain or the possible wiles of your ex, wisdom validates all the changes that are making you someone new.

> *Purity of heart is to will one thing.*
> —SOREN KIERKEGAARD

Noelle: When Dan left our home, the last thing he said was, "I'm not going to be depressed anymore." The last thing I said was, "You will take your depression with you."

I kept trying to figure things out, linking clues, piecing together fragments of knowledge, always hoping Dan would change his mind about the divorce. When he didn't, I tried to change the way I responded. When I didn't progress, he ridiculed my efforts. When I did progress, he kept saying, "You just don't get it." But I *was* beginning to get it—he knew it, and it scared him.

His only defense was projected guilt and distorting the truth. The ultimate betrayal is that Dan knowingly trampled on what was most important to me: purity of mind and body, integrity, and character. Creating sympathy for himself, he twisted the reason behind our breakup to justify his leaving. I don't blame anyone who may have believed him; after all, I believed him for 20 years. But these are abuses at the deepest level because the losses can never be validated.

Today my heart and mind are no longer ravaged; he can never rob me of a clear conscience. I know he knows the truth.

God's gift of deeper insight made me aware of the big picture and continues to illuminate my thinking. I have come so far that I am not afraid of facing the worst. I have "been there, done that," and it set me free.

It is not easy living, worshiping, and working as a divorced woman in the Christian community. You realize that in the eyes of many, your reputation is sullied. There are always those who will distrust your spirituality. But it is enough to place yourself in the light of God. No matter the brutalizing of your sexuality or femininity, no one on earth can touch your purity of heart.

More Precious Than Rubies

"Wake up!" Wisdom says. "The answers are all around you."
"Cry out for Wisdom…seek…search…find the knowledge of God."[6]

The Principal Thing

The holy wisdom of discernment and insight has nothing to do with the occult, a pathetic copy of the Creator's mystery. The occult is a counterfeit that twists evil into good, darkness into light, or bitter into sweet. Scripture says wisdom is the principal thing, more precious than rubies. Its acquisition is better than pearls. Wisdom leads the way as you perceive what you otherwise could not and you understand what otherwise is an enigma or riddle.[7]

Divorce exposes who you are in a way marriage never did. At first, you build walls for protection. But walls also keep out the good. Asking God for his wisdom will keep you installing windows that allow fresh insights and new possibilities to shine through. Disgrace is replaced with grace; your lost dignity, with glory.

"Our spiritual and emotional growth is God's 'interest' on his investment in us," say authors Henry Cloud and John Townsend. When divorce traps you in a confusing maze, wisdom leads you out. It guards the door, helping you establish healthy boundaries. It teaches who to let inside, how to say "no," and when to know the difference. According to Cloud and Townsend, "When we say 'no' to people and activities that are hurtful to us, we are protecting God's investment."[8]

A woman of insight knows who she is and does not apologize for her identity. She is like the colors of dawn pouring through a priceless Tiffany window: reflective. Beautiful. Her life is like a grand Victorian door welcoming her household and visitors from everywhere: gracious. Solid. Sound.

> *She who knows not, and knows not that she knows not, is a fool; shun her. She who knows not, and knows that she knows not, is a child; teach her. She who knows, and knows not that she knows, is asleep; wake her. She who knows, and knows that she knows, is wise; follow her.*
>
> —AUTHOR UNKNOWN

Wise Women of Discernment

As divorced people, we are not a tribe unto ourselves. Like every other human being, we like and need to be with couples. We enjoy the companionship of both old and young adults and the company of children. We often miss masculine dialogue. We have something to give as well as to receive. The body of Christ needs us as much as we need the body. Isolation in singles or midlife groups is not a healthy option.

Divorce does not mean you have been placed in God's basement. Withdrawing is not worthy of you—whether self-imposed through fear, as in Sarah Winchester's case, or imposed by the expectations of others and culture. To identify only with biblical characters whose suffering parallels your own stifles growth. You need to expand your horizons now. Look at the women who, with or without a man, took a stand and changed things.

Achsah was the daughter of Caleb, one of the original spies into the Promised Land. When her husband was not man enough to request a worthy inheritance, she did!

"Give me a blessing," she asked her father, acting from an inner sense of what was appropriate, though beyond what was customary or traditional. "Since you have given me land…give me also springs of water."[9]

Isn't that the cry of your heart, too? Your birthright is not only a piece of land, but springs that help you supply your family's needs and replenish your own emotional–spiritual cisterns. But it seems like springs don't always come with the territory. There are times when you need to boldly ask, reverencing your own worthiness in the community, in the church, and as a child of God.

> *…that the eyes of your heart may be enlightened in order that you may know the hope to which he has called you, the riches of his glorious inheritance in the saints, and his incomparably great power for us who believe.*
> —Ephesians 1:18-19 NIV

The story of another bold lady, the prophetess and judge Deborah, is related in Judges. Day after day, Deborah watched what 20 years of oppression were doing to her people. She grew tired of the harassment. Her example teaches that courage, faith, and love for God result in excellent consequences not only for ourselves, but for the people with whom we belong.

"Hasn't God promised to deliver the enemy into our hands, 900 chariots and all?" she asked a man named Barak. But it seemed no one had guts to stand against the intimidation.

"If you will go with me, then I will go," Barak said, "but if you will not go with me, I will not go!"[10]

Barak underestimated Deborah.

"Guess what—I am going!" she said. "But there'll be no glory for you! God will sell Sisera into the hand of a woman!" Deborah wasn't talking about personal glory; final victory came when a woman named Jael pegged Commander Sisera and went down in history, too. Grounded in hidden wisdom, Deborah picked up on what God wanted and went for it! Israel defeated Jabin, king of Canaan.

"Awake, awake, Deborah! Awake, awake, sing a song!" Barak and Deborah sang as praise to God. "Let those who love him be like the sun when it comes out in full strength." Her story ends with this phrase: "So the land had rest for forty years."[11]

Deborah lived in a state of grace. Her discernment brought freedom to her people. Her wakefulness radiated strength.

The sunlight is your inheritance, too. There may be no direct example of divorced women in the Bible, but that does not mean it has nothing specific to say to you. Perhaps God, respecting your personhood and dignity regardless of your marital situation, is including you in the larger picture, rather than categorizing you as married, young, old, and all ages in between. You, too, can read these passages for inspiration about how God desires to bless you as a citizen of his kingdom. Discover how he plans to use your life to continue to bless others.

> *Not to speak out against evil is to ignore the truth.*
> —Dr. Anthony Fortosis

Kari: "I walked away from the woman God gave me," Ed said the day our divorce was final. I was stunned, wondering if this was the truth...or what he *really* meant.

Though armed with textbook knowledge of midlife crisis and childhood trauma, and a few sketchy hunches, I never could justify his decision to leave his family. I'm still uncovering clues I had ignored. I may never fully know, nor do I need to.

I was raised to place my trust in parents, pastors, teachers, husband. I counted on their honesty. I had learned love is not suspicious. But dishonest people say and do exactly what it takes to lull doubts. Ed was a master at quelling my quest for truth.

During our marriage, I once telephoned him with news of a possible tumor on a mammogram and the doctor's request for repeat films. Trying to reconcile his vague response with what I'd hoped he'd say, I asked, "If this is cancer, you won't be here for me, will you?"

He said he would have to think about it.

I was paralyzed between knowing something was wrong and wanting not to know.

Another time I asked Ed to be honest about what was bothering him. He turned defensive. "Be open with me," I tried again. He told me he was dealing with me now and how to keep me happy.

My question was on target the first time; his response was phrased to get me off track.

Even Ed's tone of voice and body language were calculated to throw me off balance. I remember my anguish over how his lifestyle of arriving home late, then leaving at three in the morning, confused our daughter in the final days before he exited the family home. One night before I went to bed I taped a brief note to his lounge chair, suggesting he move out while we waited for the house to sell. He stormed into the bedroom after midnight, cursing, boasting I couldn't do anything about it, and challenging me to kick him out.

Until it happened to me, I never understood why some women stay in crazy-making relationships. To gain insight into my confusing maze, I investigated the roles in which I had been cast: Ed's surrogate mother, caretaker, and business partner; the wrongdoer; and the crazy one. I woke up. Divorce taught me to pay attention to what I value. I am not afraid to question answers. Today I know that a man who answers his wife the way Ed so often did me—squashing conversations—has serious identity issues. His harassing letters are not worth the postage stamp needed to respond. Today his responses would be unacceptable. I recognize his diversion tactics; he doesn't get away with them. Instead of being an assault on my worth, I perceive they expose his own heart.

If my mind says one thing and my spirit another, I ask myself, *What's wrong here?* I protect what's important to me, such as a peaceful house without put-downs. I shudder at Melanie's recollection of Ed's remark to her: "You only have to put up with your mother until you're 18; then you get the heck out." At that time, fear left me speechless. Now there's no more scurrying under cover because I'm afraid to speak up. No longer do I wait for "someday" to get on with my life.

Since Ed walked away, I am a much wiser woman.

> *The less you think of yourself, the more you give of yourself too freely—and the less you have left to live on.*
> —ART CIANCIO

You Are Not a Frumpy Farmhouse

Too often women guard a happy-marriage image and cover up bruises from abuse, control, and relationship manipulation. Perhaps the messages started early in childhood with, "Act like a lady." "Don't talk back." "Good girls don't…" Later they evolved into, "You're trying to make me look bad." "You provoke me." "I did it because of you." After divorce, the messages continued with, "Keep your dirty laundry to yourself." "Try to understand he means well." "It wasn't that bad; you can't prove it." "You're not perfect." "You enabled him." "Quit whining."

These messages can throw you off balance. Spirit-bruising discolors your reality and warps the truth. When someone else says that what you felt, saw, or said is not what happened, you "disintegrate." Your integrity has been "dis'ed," or invalidated. Unable to reconcile what's happening to you with what is going on out there, you doubt yourself.

Did you keep hurts a secret? Seal off part of your heart? Use up energy dodging verbal bullets or lugging his emotional baggage or ammunition? "There are two losses here to recognize," says author Patricia Evans in *The Verbally Abusive Relationship.* They are loss of love and the loss of self.

"If we were in the hands of an enemy we would know there was little or no truth in what we heard," says Evans. However a wife doesn't always "know she is being opposed for the sake of opposing." The integrity of your foundation as an infinitely valuable person has been assaulted if you were deceived, your feelings were trivialized, or things confided in privacy were twisted and used to put you down. "Learning to doubt yourself and believe something is wrong with you are all symptoms of shattered integrity," says Evans. "If a verbally abusing mate was a church leader or community pillar, the resulting confusion is doubly humiliating."[12]

Spirit- and soul-bruising does not necessarily cease with a divorce decree or restraining order. Manipulation does not scurry off to a grave. You need distance to give discernment and insight a fighting chance to free your spirit. Perhaps for the first time you now see that when you let down your hair in the safety of your home, you made yourself vulnerable. Vulnerability and trust are appropriate within marriage. If he used these to take advantage of you or they were turned against you, it is not a reflection on your integrity. Do not wound the new woman emerging by being sorry that you trusted. You no longer need to tiptoe around your own heart.

> *We carry with us the wonders we seek without us.*
> —Sir Thomas Browne

Employ Insight to Shore Up Your Boundaries

Reconstructing your perception of out-of-control situations begins when you respect your gift of discernment and your gift of insight. The gift here is an inner knowing that you know that you know that you know, even when you have no concrete evidence. Like baklava, the flaky Greek pastry made from layers of phyllo dough, you have layer upon layer of paper-thin suspicions that have accumulated through the years. Your spirit is saying, *The uneasiness is building. There's something here I need to pay attention to.*

This is not New Age thought, but a God-designed tool to preserve and protect you and the things important to you: your thoughts, values, desires, and needs; the ability to give and receive love; and even your skin (if you've been physically battered, you know what we mean).

When you are violated by a manipulator/abuser, your initial temptation is to explain it away. *I must have imagined this,* you tell yourself. *It isn't that bad.* But the uneasiness does not dissipate. You fear abandonment and don't want to admit it as a possibility. Your spirit is seeking to level the unsettling experience. Someone you loved, and you thought loved you, twisted both what you did or said and what you didn't do. You chalk it up to fatigue, stress, midlife crisis, or the devil. But beneath awareness, you know something is wrong with this picture.

Jeff Klippenes, minister and marriage–family–child counselor, freely uses the word *intuition* to refer to this gift of communication and says, "I believe it is left over from the Garden of Eden. Man and woman were transparent, knowing each other completely on a deeper level than the verbal or physical."

"We need to honor the remnant of our intuition," asserts Klippenes, "not run from it."[13] Is intuition a controversial word in the Christian community? If so, perhaps it is because we are afraid of it, the way Adam and Eve were when they knew that they were naked.[14] Intuition disrobes mysteries and reveals things as they are. But in the context of sin, it frightens people and makes them hide.

Looking back at the Garden, we see how Satan cunningly confused Eve's clarity of mind and discounted her insight about God's will by telling a lie concealed in a truth. Eve lost her integrity (wholeness) the day she and her mate ate the fruit of the tree of the knowledge of good and evil. Since then all humanity lives under the shadow of death and we see "through a glass, darkly."[15]

The exercise of insight and discernment, or the intuition Klippenes refers to, may be what Paul refers to as "comparing spiritual things with spiritual." He previously describes God's wisdom as "hidden," spoken in a "mystery," saying, "God has revealed them to us through His Spirit. For the Spirit searches all things, yes, the deep things of God...that we might know the things that have been freely given to us by God."[16] You do not need to fully understand why you are feeling what you are feeling in order to put deeper insight to work performing reality checks. We often leave deeper insight/intuition on the shelf of our experience to gather dust because we can't scientifically prove or theologically explain it to ourselves or others. But that does not mean truth cannot be discerned.

Building Tips

Join the 15 million female homeowners now picking up hammer and nails. Handy hardware includes a good hammer, tape measure, Vise-Grip (locking) pliers, Crescent (adjustable-end) wrench, utility knife, several screwdrivers (Phillips head and regular), an assortment of nails, and a sturdy six-foot ladder.

The writer of Proverbs counseled, "Trust in the LORD with all your heart, and lean not on your own understanding."[17] He was aware that relying on your mental faculties alone is not enough in this hazy world. You are to trust in someone higher whose Spirit, like yours, will not fit within the small box of your own understanding. The Spirit of God leads you into truth[18] when you are ready to receive it.

The story about Jesus walking on water records that the disciples "were utterly astonished" when Jesus climbed in the boat with them. Why? Because "they had not gained any insight from the incident of the loaves, but their heart was hardened." We may not be in a position to handle learning the truth that insight brings. We forget that Solomon, the wisest man, discovered that "in much wisdom there is much grief, and increasing knowledge results in increasing pain."[19] Sometimes we don't want to know the truth. God may wait until we are ready and able to handle it.

Wisdom is God's delight that begins when we fear him.[20] But to get there, most of us take the circuitous route through the maze of our own understanding. Wanting quick answers and solutions, we forget that knowing him is a process. Can we fully understand what he is doing, when, or why? *The Living Bible* paraphrase of 1 Corinthians 2:14-16 puts it this way:

> Only those who have the Holy Spirit within them can understand what the Holy Spirit means. Others just can't take it in. But the spiritual man has insight into everything, and that bothers and baffles the man of the world, who can't understand him at all. How could he? For certainly he has never been one to know the Lord's thoughts, or to discuss them with him, or to move the hands of God by prayer. But, strange as it seems, we Christians actually do have within us a portion of the very thoughts and mind of Christ.

God wants access into you in order to free you from the intimidation you feel in the presence of a controller. Throw open the sashes of your spirit. Invite the light in. Pick up on nuances in the other person's innuendos. Hear every word he doesn't say. Listen for the "aha" in your spirit. We dare you.

Think sideways!

—EDWARD DE BONOS

Dare 1: Cut yourself some slack. Manipulation and abuse are cumulative. Each encounter with a controller tilts you further off your rocker, an integral part of that person's agenda. You're led into a maze of helplessness where you can't explain why you feel upset (angry, confused, hysterical, depressed) or act out (yell, cry, slam cupboards, throw things). Where you can't decipher what is happening or connect past incidents to today's, find a quiet place. Take a deep breath. Cut yourself some slack.

Dare 2: Welcome your rising annoyance, that off-balance sensation. It is there as a warning. Wake up to signals in your body language; you stiffen or slump, you clench your jaw. Notice how your fear places the manipulator in control; he counts on emotional shock waves to leave you reeling. Think about this. Respond accordingly.

Dare 3: Watch for attack-and-evasion techniques. Manipulators are skilled at their agenda. They tap your soft spots, including your fear of hurting another's feelings. They motivate by projecting false guilt that you can do more—so when you drop your guard, you will nurse their wounds or handle their responsibilities. They listen for your vulnerabilities, then use them to stab you later.

Dare 4: Just say "no." Catch your initial defensive reaction to say too much or not enough. Decide in favor of a neutral, nonthreatening environment. Simply walk away. If you stay and things get out of hand, calmly say, "I refuse to be treated like that." You can choose where you want to live emotionally.

Dare 5: Accept the risks. Waking up to the truth doesn't mean others will change or stick around; manipulators will abandon you if they don't get their way. Expect it. "Sometimes setting boundaries clarifies that you were left a long time ago, in every way, perhaps, except physically," says John Townsend. "Boundaries are a 'litmus test' for the qualities of our relationships. Those who can't respect our boundaries are telling us that they don't love our 'no.' They only love our 'yes,' or compliance."[21]

Dare 6: Consider this remodeling tip from Sarah Winchester's life— never let fear seal off your inner house; it also shuts out the light. History is a credible teacher. Let past manipulative/abusive experience reveal your need to intuit in future relationships. As you

boldly step across the threshold toward a new you, in time you
will learn again to trust yourself, God, and trustworthy others.

> *I have come back again to where I belong;*
> *Not an enchanted place, but the walls are strong.*
> —DOROTHY H. RATH

Kari: For too long I abdicated my good sense. Divorce helped
me see I had allowed Ed to take away parts of myself that God
values. I'd been taught to please, often apologizing simply to avoid
conflict. "I'm a different person now," I told my mother. "You may
not like what you hear coming out of my mouth." I'm not sure
she understood that I'm discovering a person I never allowed myself
to be.

I was still gullible at times—sometimes denial appeared the eas-
iest route—but I made progress. I enrolled in a management class
on dealing with difficult people and began to understand that defer-
ring to another's wishes isn't necessarily an act of love. Saying "no"
to a co-worker or boss, a church committee or someone signifi-
cant in my life, doesn't mean I'm not honoring God.

I got over the criticism leveled at me that I'm self-absorbed if
I draw a line or if I walk away and refuse to engage toxic people.
Never again do I want to lose myself because I fear speaking up.
No more whitewashing of demeaning remarks disguised as jokes.
Living free from fear of what others think, being able to trust, and
honoring my pure heart are important to me. I need people in my
life who allow me to do that, who value my independent thoughts,
appreciate my talents, and encourage the hopes and respect the
desires God has placed in my heart. I conserve my emotional energy
to bless the world, not just pacify at any price.

> *Eye has not seen, nor ear heard, nor have entered into the heart of man the things which God has prepared for those who love Him.*
>
> —1 CORINTHIANS 2:9

You Are a Mansion

Wisdom teaches that what you came to believe were your failings are in actuality your gifts. Now you recognize things as they really are. When you tolerated more, committed to loving in spite of pain, and retreated to keep the peace, your partner perceived it as weakness and used it to his advantage. Your perceptions were not validated. Part of the recovery of the spirit is realizing what was going on under the surface.

For example, if you never felt accepted by your mate, a legitimate human need was not being met. It is a valid loss. Spiritual recovery and nourishment comes as your spirit validates your needs, rights, and losses. Discernment is the conscious acknowledgment of what your spirit already knows. When you integrate the loss into your life experience, you obtain wisdom. Each step takes you to the next. You lost love, but you did not lose yourself—permanently. Your self-esteem can be torn down, but never your self-worth.

Finish the Unfinished

Remember Luci Baines Johnson? The daughter of President Lyndon Johnson dropped out of college to marry and then raised four children. After a divorce and remarriage, she promised herself that by age 50 she'd have a university degree. "It was time to finish unfinished business," she says. In 1997, the year her son Lyndon graduated from law school, she earned her diploma, with 69 credits given for "life experience."[22]

From now on, refuse to leave your spirit unguarded. Let no one trample your perceptions or discount your feelings. Clutch the sword of the Spirit: truth. You have a purpose to accomplish and need your wits about you to complete what God said he will finish in and through you.

You are not asked to lose yourself to the extent that you have nothing left to live on. Biblical submission is not about someone else controlling you in Jesus' name. Both women and men, living in the same household of faith as children of the king, are called to serve the other.[23] An escape clause was not drawn up for either gender. Get to know exploitation techniques that discount, divert, and deny your reality (see pages 209–210).

> *Behold, I send you out as sheep in the midst of wolves.*
> *Therefore be wise as serpents and harmless as doves.*
> —MATTHEW 10:16

Noelle: Truth always surfaces. As I kept listening to my spirit, seeking insight, three dramatic instances of revelation brought my understanding of what was really happening to a climax. I do not know why the Holy Spirit chose to reveal what he did when he did—once through a dream and twice through supernatural knowledge. I had no evidence, no way of knowing about the long term double life of my spouse at that time. Only after I confronted my ex did he acknowledge it.

Initially, the revelations were mind-boggling, horrendously painful. I'm glad now that my eyes were enlightened. Instead of forever blaming myself, I saw clearly why I kept hitting walls in prayer and got nowhere in my desire to renew intimacy and rejuvenate our marriage. God will not change another person's will.

When the light exposed the bigger picture of multiple infidelity, I was able to disconnect emotionally from my ex and move forward. No amount of pleading would change anything if he chose not to address the issues. Now I realize that where deception, addiction, and manipulation are at work, human knowledge does not suffice.

When Dan and The Neighbor broke up, he used the news as an opportunity to apologize for hurting me. But inconsistencies in his story were warning lights. Later, my discovery that even those details were couched in lies confirmed what had taken me so long to figure out. The breach of trust was complete. That's when I heard God saying, "Follow me, and let the dead bury their own dead."[24]

I want to be an open window, to let light put out the darkness, to discern more than before in ongoing communication with my ex. To hear the difference between what is real and what is phony. I want what happened to me to be part of what God uses to help others.

> *The God of our Lord Jesus Christ, the Father of Glory...*
> *give to you the spirit of wisdom and revelation in the*
> *knowledge of Him, the eyes of your understanding being*
> *enlightened.*
> —EPHESIANS 1:17-18

A Multifaceted Woman

Esther was a gorgeous Tiffany window. She was the embodiment of mystique, which is, according to Merriam–Webster's, "an air or attitude of mystery or reverence developing around something or someone." Through her life, light spilled upon straw floors of a peasant's hut and the rare wall coverings and richly carpeted floors of the royal palace. Scripture says she obtained favor with everyone who saw her. In those days, more than ever, a woman's face was her fortune. But Esther knew sex appeal is not an external look but is expressed from the inside out. She won the queen of Persia beauty contest without requesting special favors. Her passion for life was her greatest asset. It led to her destiny: the opportunity to save her Jewish race and culture.

Esther knew who she was and where she'd come from, and she kept her identity intact in a foreign land. She was discerning and insightful—a woman who didn't display all her cards at one time. She allowed mystique to be the trump card.

Esther did not hurry. She built in time. To paraphrase a Kenny Rogers song, "she knew when to hold 'em, knew when to fold 'em." When told she had to appeal to her husband to spare her people, at first she wanted to refuse the assignment. Though she was married to the king, she was well aware that approaching his throne without an invitation meant death. Finally she realized the Jews' safety was worth any price. "If I perish, I perish!" she said.[25]

Commanding her people to pray diligently, she pondered how to win the king's attention. First she exchanged her fasting clothes for fancy royal robes. When the king welcomed her into his presence, she boldly invited him for dinner without saying why. At the banquet, she changed her mind about telling him yet. "Come again tomorrow," she said. Esther was cooking up courage, or perhaps building his interest by inviting him for more than one night.

Esther was complex. Her life held many paradoxes: poverty and riches, duty and glory, fear and courage. She balanced these and let her full humanity shine through. Being multifaceted is about recognizing how far you've come, celebrating your gifts and paradoxes, and living up to your potential in the kingdom.

> *Sing, O childless woman! Break out into loud and joyful song...for she who was abandoned has more blessings now than she whose husband stayed! Enlarge your house; build on additions; spread out your home! For you will soon be bursting at the seams!...Fear not; you will no longer live in shame...For your Creator will be your "husband."...For the Lord has called you back from your grief—a young wife abandoned by her husband.*
>
> —ISAIAH 54:1-6 TLB

Like Esther, you, too, can allow mystique to be the trump card in both perilous and predictable situations. How you view what happens to you in life determines what you reflect to others. Mystique is an attitude you choose to convey, like aging gracefully or dying with dignity. It's the same with divorce. You can go through it reluctantly, sheepishly, or with grace. How you do it becomes your style. Maybe it's as elusive as a twinkle in your eye, a knowing nod of the head, a smile. It shows in your tone of voice, the thrust of your jaw, the drop of your shoulders. Mystique displays the way you personally relate to your circumstances. Reverence for yourself and for what has happened to you means you respect the refining process of life's losses with a curtsy.

"Mystique can be learned," said women's issues expert Jean Lush, author of *The Emotional Phases of a Woman's Life*, "often with great effort, but it's not that some are born with it and some are not."[26] This air of reverence about you cannot be defined or formulated, just as God's character cannot be defined. As soon as you try to explain it or list ten easy steps to get it, it's not there anymore.

Why do some women seem to have more of it than others? We don't know. It is a quality that defies our ability to categorize. Similar to fragrance, it goes where you go and leaves the lingering scent in the air of who you are and what you've been through. It is like taking your own bouquet of garden-picked roses to the deli for lunch. A room that before smelled of dill pickles is now filled with a fragrant essence. People notice. Mystique is like that. You can carry ambience with you and are not dependent on others to create it or provide it. The mystique of roses and yourself is that thorns are inherent, the difficulties are part of your value now, part of what make you whole, integral, enhancing the world.

Isabella Rossellini says, "There is some unknown force that makes us move all together in one direction or another, toward a given style. It's a fascinating mystery."[27] Perhaps this mystery of reverence is a remnant of being created in the image of God; a remnant of his sweet presence in our earthy, sometimes paltry, lives. As such, it is your birthright as a woman and child of God. Like Esther, you are a window. Through your life God wants to spill light into the mystery of circumstance. You, too, are in a scary place. But you are heading toward your destiny, a new place and a new time. A new you.

> *Here I am! I stand at the door and knock. If you hear my voice and open the door, I will come in and eat with you, and you will eat with me.*
> —REVELATION 3:20 NCV

His Threshold

In divorce, as in Sarah Winchester's house, there are many doors. You want to open them but sometimes are timid or afraid. What will you find? Deeper insight? An air of reverence about you that you never knew you had? Increased authenticity? Finely tuned discernment? When will God next do something incredible in and through you? Soon you see he's at the door. Sooner or later you'll find he *is* the door.[28] Boldly step across the threshold. It's time to say, "Look out, world! I like the new me."

Start anew!

Now is the time to...

Heart Work

- try tofu
- pierce my ears or belly button
- plant turnips or roses
- go on a blind date
- return to college
- write a book

Words to the Wise About Verbal Exploitation

It takes two to tangle: one vulnerable person and another who exploits through inappropriate use of emotional power. A manipulator locates vulnerability by trial and error and then uses that knowledge to distress and bring pressure to bear. Protect your tender heart. Because you don't easily recognize when you are being overpowered, awareness of your vulnerable spots is imperative.

- *Your feelings are discounted and undermined.* When he says, "You make a big deal out of nothing/can't take a joke/always complain/take things too seriously/jump to conclusions/blow it out of proportion," you feel insecure, confused, invalidated; you fear disapproval, want to appease, conform, or both. His intention is to insinuate that your feelings are bad, instead of neutral and worth talking about.

- *You are diverted from the real issues.* When he says—"Just drop it/get off my back/give me space/chill out; you heard me/know what I meant/always have to be right"—you are getting too close to the truth. He can't afford to face it or feel his feelings, is afraid of conflict and anger, makes himself the victim.

- *You are blamed and criticized.* When he says, "You're looking for trouble/always take the last word/are never satisfied/have expectations that are too big/wouldn't understand/don't get it/think you're so smart," you feel irrationally guilty, in denial, selfish, traumatized by nagging; he knows exactly how much resistance will be offered before you break down.

- *You are controlled by silence, withdrawal, forgetting.* When he says, "Whatever you say, dear/it'll be all right/wait and see/I don't have to listen to this/you're making that up/you heard me wrong/I have to go…" (door slams), you feel worn down by his absence, played against someone else, at a dead end, given no option but to protest in nonverbal ways. He then uses those to invalidate, blame, and divert you in an ongoing cycle, saying things like, "You make a big deal out of nothing."

What you can do about verbal exploitation:

- *Maintain objectivity.* Don't allow anyone to make you assume things that are not true.

- *Recognize things he says that arouse feelings of powerlessness and confusion.* Use them as cues to be cautious and wary.

- *Process flashbacks,* because when you recognize your vulnerable spots and what was used against you in the past, you gain insight.

- *Be alert when he plays the blame-and-shame game.* You don't have to defend yourself or dignify his criticism with a response.

- *If you feel uncomfortable with any comment,* it is a red flag to walk away.

Chapter Fourteen

My Children Are Listening

I will watch over them to build and to plant, says the LORD.
In those days they shall say no more: "The fathers have eaten
sour grapes, and the children's teeth are set on edge."

—JEREMIAH 31:28-29

Noelle: I disliked roller coasters. But Space Mountain loomed like a personal challenge in my own "Tomorrowland." I'd taken my daughters to Disneyland for the Christmas holidays just weeks after Dan announced his intention to leave. Throughout Frontierland and Fantasyland, I tried hard not to lose it, but the pain of why we were doing this was getting to me. In Tomorrowland, I forced back more tears as we moseyed through each labyrinth, waiting our turn at the rides. Finally, the line led into a huge, dark cavern. We couldn't see each other's faces. How I welcomed a place to finally let my tears spill, my sniffling covered by the rattle and rumble of machinery and distant screams.

As the girls and I climbed aboard our spaceship, I noticed a sign warned of danger for pregnant women and people with heart conditions. *The rougher the better*, I thought. *Maybe I'll miscarry this terrible trauma.*

Then, off we went, picking up speed. Each turn and twist came as a surprise because the entire ride was taking place in blackout-simulated outer space. As the ship careened around the first deep curve, a sickening fear rose in my gut.

Pay attention, something told me. I heard clearly formed sentences: *You are going to feel completely out of control. This is a metaphor for your life right now. Don't be afraid. Go with each bump and jolt. Lean into the rolls and rushes. Don't resist. God is with you.* It was rough. It was tough. But the scariest part of that ride was getting out, jostled and windblown, into the glare of reality. I knew the ride of my life had just begun.

> *So take a new grip with your tired hands, stand firm on your shaky legs.*
> —HEBREWS 12:12 TLB

The Mother of All Rides

Hop aboard! Single-parenting while recovering from the derailment of a long-term marriage is the mother of all roller-coaster rides. But you can do it. It starts when you're newly divorced, financially challenged, and scared to death. At the same time, you do any or all of these: work full-time, job-hunt, taxi your child to school events, attend parent–teacher conferences, help with homework, research day care, do the bills, clean house, wash laundry, volunteer for field trips, teach Sunday school, and try to find time for a bath. All the while, you are handling your own grief.

Are you at the end of your rope? Yes. Alone? No. In our country, most one-parent homes are headed by women, increasing from

3 million such cases in 1970 to 10 million in 2000, according to the U.S. Census Bureau. Since the 1960s the percentage of children living apart from their biological fathers has roughly doubled. Tonight, nearly 50 percent of American children may be going to sleep without being able to say good night to their dads. But single motherhood has lost much of its stigma, and today's single mother doesn't fit the old stereotype. We are better-educated and are able to provide for ourselves. "Lone parenthood is not generally a selfish and willful choice," states the Joseph Rowntree Foundation of Britain, "and children in lone-parent families are not neglected and undisciplined."[1]

Sometimes the more you know, the scarier it gets. Other times darkness acts as a cover to keep you from anticipating each jolt of the journey. You'll twist and turn through guilt, mistakes, and humiliation. Take each curve as it comes: your children testing you (they may appear resilient but have a pocketful of resentment—or the opposite). Your ex-spouse outwitting you (he may undermine your authority). The other woman taunting you (she may threaten your position as role model). Relatives or friends misunderstanding you (they may offer hurtful advice).

Lean into the turns. Expect the unexpected. Prepare for the unpredictable. You are a remarkable human being with a desire to do the best you can. You can be your own hero. Write your own success story. Practice tumbling, sinking, rising. You'll land safely at the end.

> *It's not easy being a mother. If it were, fathers would do it.*
>
> —DOROTHY, *THE GOLDEN GIRLS*

Kari: The day I moved into single-parenting, I was weighted with more than cardboard boxes. *Whose pain do I deal with first?* I wondered. *Sometimes Melanie is like an enemy in my own camp.* Once I thought, *I've lost her.*

Her history and past family traditions had crumbled. Nothing stayed the same. For example, birthdays and holidays were negotiated. "I feel like I have to choose," she said. The first Mother's Day after the divorce, she dined in a fancy restaurant with daddy and girlfriend. "She's so pretty," I was told when Melanie returned. "She'd make a better mother than you." (Was I glad I was treating myself to monthly counseling sessions!)

I Can Do This!

Counselors recommend the following guidelines for raising children during the first year after a divorce:

- Expect anger, and establish a safe zone for venting it.
- Be prepared for tough questions. Answer briefly and age-appropriately.
- Do as much as you can together: chores, play, naps, creative projects.
- Make affection a daily habit, even if the children shrug it off.
- Accept that you can't control what they do with your ex-spouse.
- Minimize changes in your schedule, neighborhood, church.
- Make your dating a low priority at first; allow children time to adjust.
- Affirm and reassure your children that the divorce is not their fault.

As a mother I was taking such a beating that I needed my cup filled back up. Twice yearly, my mother visited, scenting our kitchen with roasting turkey and creamy noodles. My father repaired the roof. Melanie and I felt cozy and cared for. But I knew I needed someone to talk to other times, when Melanie would say, "At Daddy's place I don't have to clean my room or dig dandelions. And we always stop for pizza." It seemed as if Ed was always trying to throw me off balance. He also used information from her to rearrange my plans on the weekends Melanie was supposed to be with him. Thank goodness my friend Regina taught me to be proactive. "Always have plan B and C," she said. That meant a babysitter on call when a weekend visitation was cancelled and I had my own activities arranged.

Mary, my second mom, telephoned weekly. "What's going on?" she'd ask. I filled her ears with Melanie's visitation tales, such as "trolling for women" with her dad. I ranted, *"How dare he?"*

One Friday night, friends had to scrape me off the ceiling with a spatula. "I want to come home, Mom. Can you pick me up?" Twelve-year-old Melanie was calling from a bar while she was with her dad for the weekend. The parenting rules I had relied on no longer worked. My days seemed to race further out of control.

Then there were those with this advice: "Put Melanie in a foster home." "Give her to her dad." And, "No man will ever want to marry you with your daughter around." Regardless of these comments, I couldn't think of walking away.

Several months later my resolve was confirmed. I ran into a business acquaintance I had once worked with. "If your daughter makes it," he said, "it will be with you. You're the best parent for the job."

I committed for the long haul, living what I believe and refusing to play the popularity game. "I can't compete with 'Popcorn Daddy' by giving you everything you want," I once told my daughter. "All

I can give you is what I think you need: a love that knows how to say 'no.' The stability of a home you can call your own. Consistency, whether you think I'm old-fashioned or mean. Values like taking responsibility and believing that being a good person is more important than feeling good."

> *We experience moments absolutely free from worry. These brief respites are called panic.*
>
> —CULLEN HIGHTOWER

Peanut-Brittle Moments

Children of divorce face a terrifying task—understanding why the parents who love, protect, and care for them are causing them distress, fear, confusion, and anger. Children are a reminder that you and their dad once had a history together, like a solid block of peanut brittle now broken into jagged bits. Whose shattering do you handle first? Theirs or yours?

"When a marriage breaks down, most men and women experience a diminished capacity to parent," writes Judith Wallerstein in *Second Chances*, a book about who wins, who loses, and why. "They give less time, provide less discipline, and are less sensitive to their children, being caught up themselves in the personal maelstrom of divorce and its aftermath. Many parents are temporarily unable to separate their children's needs from their own."[2]

According to Wallerstein, a psychologist with more than a quarter-century of research behind her, "The single most important protective factor in a child's psychological development and well-being over the years is the mother's mental health and the quality of her parenting." (Go ahead, scream!) But, she says, "The time that you invest in comforting your children, in being available to them in the evenings, is the most important investment you can make in your future relationship with them."[3]

With another psychologist, Joan B. Kelly, Wallerstein discovered that adolescents in psychological difficulty at the time of divorce lacked the inner integration necessary to face complex demands. Others increased in maturity and independence through greater responsibility, not only for themselves, but temporarily for their troubled parents.[4] The authors stress that the central hazard for the child is not his own unhappiness, but the family disruption that may discourage or interfere with his developmental progress, or move him into a phase for which he is not ready.

Eight Promises to My Children

- I will try to be the best parent I can be.
- I will make time during the week just for you.
- I will take good care of myself well, so I can better care for you.
- I will allow you to be my child, not expect you to be my caregiver.
- I will be available to you anytime; I'll expect the same courtesy of you.
- I will model the values I talk about: fairness, honesty, forgiveness.
- I will not speak against your dad. I'll apologize when I do.
- I will get up one more time than I'm knocked down.

(P.S.—When I try and fail, please forgive me. I love you.)

"You never get over it; you just get on with it," the saying goes. This is never so true as with children of divorce. Too much is dumped into their laps at one time. They have no context for dealing with the load. They don't know what to do with their emotions or how to cope with potential changes that for them mean big losses. Some children get stuck emotionally at the age they experienced paternal abandonment.

The stakes of parenting are higher now. The children need affirmation and reassurance. They want both parents at home under the same roof and are coping with their frustration in individual ways. If you have more than one child, the dilemma is doubled or quadrupled. One wants to be good but can't help being bad. Another tries to provoke you, all the time hoping to be accepted and approved. A third appears cool but burns with resentment. A fourth lets out all his hostility, then curls up and cries himself to sleep.

Never be embarrassed by your sweaty palms during this unsteady ride. As you try your hardest in what looks like a heartbreaking situation, heed the best-parent rule: *Surround yourself with people who reinforce your values, embrace your personhood, and encourage you to be the best you can be.* It may be a friend, family member, or someone you pay $70 an hour to listen to you.

What looks like the worst may be a sign that better is yet to come. Forget about tickets for smoother, slower rides. Hold on to your seat for the duration. Your children count on it.

> *I can't go on like this. (But until circumstances change,
> I probably will.)*
> —AUTHOR UNKNOWN

Noelle: "I realize this is not a bad way to live," said my middle child, "just different." She had relished the times Dan was there to tuck her in at night. He had placed the first paintbrush into her slender, artistic fingers. She had found security in his presence.

After I became the custodial parent, Dan eventually moved away. She was 14 when he left and, of the three, appeared least able to adjust, in spite of the gentle wisdom she expressed so well at times.

Although we had blowouts, I learned from her that my children are listening. They tune in to each word I say and everything I don't say. They notice changing voice inflections and watch body language. They pick up subtle and direct slips of the tongue.

From the beginning, they'd tell me, "Mom, don't! I don't need to know that. He's still my dad, and I'm gonna love him anyway." I got better at respecting their need to honor their father. But I drew up short when it came to The Neighbor.

Until the divorce, my children had never heard me swear or utter obscenities. "Girls, there are times when obscenity is appropriate," I told them now. Here in the reality of my hurt, they saw the raw, gritty side of me. Perhaps the fact I didn't cover it up validated their own feelings that divorce is crazy. Instead of wilting in divorce, I reacted, because I wanted to live.

One of my friends laughed and helped me not take my new self so seriously. Others quipped, "You're only hurting yourself." Looking back, I think if I had acted differently I would have been lying to myself and to my daughters. I wanted to communicate a sense of moral discernment in a world that puts a spin on the Word of God by saying "judge not" when an ethical or moral dilemma is presented. Maybe I didn't do it in the best way, but I modeled reality: that faithfulness is fundamental. What my husband did was outrageous. Deception and betrayal destroy something precious inside a woman and her children. Seduction ruins many lives. I pray it will never happen to my children, and more importantly, I pray that they will never be a party to any other couple's divorce.

I always wondered how an acquaintance of mine maintained emotional and spiritual equilibrium throughout her ordeal. I struggled with her banal sweetness until I discovered it was not as it appeared. She was dying inside. I knew that when the Space Mountain ride was over I didn't want to be a "ghost woman" like her. I wanted to seize the lows and soar the heights—and not be scared of the ups and downs of the wildest ride. "Let's do it again!" the girls and I shouted that sunny California day.

"And then," I answered, "let's head for Six Flags Magic Mountain!" I'd heard about "Superman: the Escape"—a roller coaster that goes from 0 to 100 miles per hour in seven seconds. Now I look back and wonder if even the thrill of its free fall—the world's fastest—would top the rush of that first year as a single mom!

> *Children are a great deal more apt to follow your lead than the way you point.*
> —ANONYMOUS

Lemonade-Stand Love

"If you are feeling sad [or mad] and tell a child that 'everything is fine,' you are giving a double message," says Isolina Ricci, author of *Mom's House, Dad's House*.[5] She declares that demystification of events is very important. "Better to admit, 'I'm sad [or mad] right now,' and then reassure the child, 'But it's not about you and me. It's about grown-up matters.'" Ricci believes it is easier for children to deal with the truth than confront whispered hostility, martyred silences, or actions that contradict words.

You know everything is not "fine." Divorce and child-custody laws are in a state of flux. The system appears stacked against women and children. Once California passed the first "no-fault" divorce bill in 1969 and 49 states followed, the number of divorces in this country surged 68 percent.

"It is legally easier to divorce your spouse of 26 years than it is to fire someone you hired last week," says Randal Helman, a former judge and executive of the Michigan Family Forum, a group that lobbies for divorce-law reform.[6]

Under no-fault law, one partner's desire to end the marriage supersedes the other's desire to keep it intact. The balance of power favors the divorce seeker, even if that person has been having an affair, has abandoned his or her family, or both. Some lawyers say women have lost the opportunity to negotiate more favorable financial settlements. (In contrast, others claim a system based on fault stacks the deck against the party with less economic power—usually the woman.)[7]

All moms are at risk: Some lose custody if they are too successful; others if they aren't. Attorney Marcia Clark's ex-husband sued for custody of their two sons because she was "too busy working." As you navigate your own dark labyrinth, you give your children what you can. Some ex-spouses are congenial; others, controlling; a few, conniving. You work with what you get, and you pray for what you need. You leave the unfairness of it all and your inability to right the wrong with someone stronger.[8] You hold together what's left of family. You compromise with your betrayer to protect and provide for your children.

Getting caught in power struggles with your children about how nice Daddy's condo is or how much he spends entertaining them impedes progress. It wastes precious emotional energy. It's time to convey the most important message to your children: "I care about you." Focus on communicating that you cannot give them what you and they most want: an intact family. Your children will ask questions and express confusion. Just be there. As you wave goodbye to what will never be again, you are promising to never say, "I can't help you," and to always say, "I'll do what I can."

How to Make Lemonade out of a Lemon

- If you tend to get emotional or flustered, avoid face-to-face meetings with your ex.

- Set up phone appointments, at your convenience, so you're not caught off guard. Before the call, list points you want to cover.

- Keep your tone strictly business. Hang up before the conversation gets personal or either of you becomes emotional, angry, or irrational.

- Focus on the children's wishes and welfare.

- Avoid making your ex's problems yours. Do not seek empathy for your own. Refuse to mother him.

- Do not be the go-between for your children and your ex or allow your children to be the go-between for you and their father.

Kari: My daughter is grown now and living on her own. She completed college with a graduate degree. I'm proud of how far she has come. But our life together after the divorce was not without residuals.

Now I know: Divorce ends a marriage but does not terminate a family. For years, Melanie's father was always present in our lives—in visits with her, occasional letters, phone calls, memories, and even fantasy. He was her idol. No wonder I experienced so much resistance from her in the early years. It took days to return to normal living after she came back from Wednesday-night outings and every other weekend at his place. Sometimes she was arrogant, authoritarian, and verbally abusive.

"I'm being the best parent I can," I often told Melanie. When I no longer had energy to argue over homework, I allowed her to fail high-school algebra the first time through. When she returned from a sixteenth-birthday trip with her dad and said, "I'm going on a blind date Friday, like it or not," I arrived at a turning point.

Melanie already knew the parameters around her dating: Mom meets the boy and whoever drives. This time she vehemently objected and said that her dad had joint custody—he had given her permission because she needed to be in a serious relationship by the time she was 18. Although I could not rush the settling of her agitated emotions or hold back the fear that stormed my heart, I refused to be held hostage any longer in my own home.

I pulled out her suitcase and said, "Then your dad can have total responsibility for raising you. I won't watch you destroy yourself and pick up the pieces afterward." Her door slammed. I trembled. She stayed.

Now there is little she and I can't talk about. Finally, she saw that home and family aren't about perfect people...but about listening ears, loving hearts, and warm hugs. She caught on that whatever happens, her mom is her biggest fan.

For me, single-parenting coincided with her teenage years. Some of the harrowing adventure would have happened without the divorce. But does a mother ever get over how divorce hurts her child? As Psalm 69:4 says, "Though I have stolen nothing, I still must restore it." By staying through the topsy-turvy ride, I hope I've showed Melanie the way home.

Wrapping Up the Holidays

When you're pacing the floor because holiday weekends are too quiet or you have nowhere to go, remember that it's a fallacy that the whole world has a date on New Year's eve, receives valentines in February, and serves Easter brunch. What to do when family-packed SUVs and boats pull out of neighborhood driveways on summer holidays? Sit in the sun on your back porch or nap in the shade. And on Thanksgiving or Christmas? Wallpaper over those Currier and Ives images. Curl up on the couch with a great classic video, or chuckle at Chevy Chase in *Christmas Vacation*, thankful all those creatures aren't stirring in your house!

> *Who takes a child by the hand, takes a mother by the heart.*
>
> —OLD PROVERB

Noelle: After my divorce, I didn't do little girls' birthday parties anymore (or help with math homework). My mothering was no longer based on things like that. My kids would no longer do picnics or camp with me. Our bonding experiences as a family began to be based on radically different criteria. I clung to the belief that the early years mattered more than I realized at the time. I would constantly ask myself, "How can I facilitate activities together that my children enjoy?"

Meanwhile, I carried on watering the lawn, stocking the fridge, attending each of my girls' sport events. Some days I looked around and marveled, saying right out loud, "I'm still here!" I was the parent who was getting up in the morning to the sound of their alternative music, starting the fire in the woodstove, maintaining their home, paying the bills, quelling emotional brushfires; cheering on the pole-vaulter, the volleyball player, and two different basketball teams; waiting up nights, and handing out hugs whether they wanted one or not. All without getting burned out, beat up, or bled dry. Anybody who wants to can criticize me, blame me, accuse me of anything they want. But I'm still here. That fact speaks with more eloquence than anything else I could possibly say. (So I won't.)

> *The greatest ability is dependability.*
>
> —ANONYMOUS

On the Right Track

Not one single mom we've talked to says the ride is smooth. Maybe you are hitting the big curves right now. You are always defending your actions and reactions. You're not a failure. You are doing the best you can. Nobody else can fill your seat. You keep focused on being the best parent you can be. In the end, that's what counts.

Write Your Own Prayer

Heart Work

I wrote the following prayer and in my mind, saw myself giving my child to my ex. *He's won*, I thought then. But my relinquishment of her freed God to work. Holding her up to him helped me move on, caring better for myself so I could care better for her.

Dear God,

I feel tired. It's 11:35 PM. Tonight I commit to you my daughter. I'm afraid of what's happening. I see her out of control. It is hard to deal with a daughter I dearly love but do not like, and who does not like me or want to be with me. My health is at risk over this tension. My life feels on hold until this question is resolved. What should I do, Lord? You've brought me through anguish unbelievable, and now I have a new problem. I turn this over to you. Help me let go, trust you, and wait patiently for you to work. I place my trembling hand in yours and look ahead, not back. I know you have a plan. Help me not to miss it. Thank you for your answers!

I love you, Lord.

Kari

Write your own prayer as you picture yourself giving your child back to God.

Holidays? Do More Than Survive!

You'll thrive a little more each year as you implement these tips:

- If an old tradition fits your new life, repeat it. If it doesn't feel right or there is pain when you think of it, replace it.

- Do something outrageous. Rent an RV and take off for the desert, work at an inner-city shelter, bundle up for a New Year's walk on the beach.

- Make excuses for parties: last day of autumn, a child's driver's license, tax returns filed, a child's report card.

- Adopt a theme for your home. Call it the Year of Light or Year of Simplicity. Give your walls a fresh coat of paint and string tiny lights afterwards.

- Get input from your children as you create new ways to celebrate their birthdays. Mingle those with familiar traditions.

- Keep a journal of holidays, including what worked and what didn't. Stimulate new ideas for next year.

- Redefine Valentine's Day. If your heart is still bleeding, express your love for yourself in art. Write a message affirming the woman you are.

- Start one new tradition and one new recipe for each holiday this year.

- Fill your home with music, ambience, good smells. Make the atmosphere work and you won't have to.

- Plant a dormant amaryllis bulb and watch hope sprout.

Chapter Fifteen
I'm Laughing Again

He will yet fill your mouth with laughter and your lips with shouts of joy.

—JOB 8:21 TLB

⁓☙☙⁓

She stood in the doorway watching him. He didn't see her until he closed the car door. In the silvery moonlight, slender shadows danced on the slick icy sidewalk. Billy Boy strolled into the house.

"Come on in," said Sandra Sue. "I've been waiting for you." With a toss of her long blond mane, she smiled.

Billy Boy could see in those baby-blue eyes and luscious lips that Sandra Sue meant business. "I've come for what's mine," he said.

"I know, Babe," she said, sauntering toward the stairway.

"Take it off," Billy Boy said, pointing to her creamy velour robe. "Half of everything's mine—including your clothes."

"Fine," said Sandra Sue. "No problem." She dropped the robe at his feet and climbed the stairs. "You know where my closet is. Go ahead. See what fits!" Her silhouette disappeared behind the shower door.

Later, Billy Boy drove into the sunset with his pop-tart by his side and half the "community" property in the trunk of his BMW. Sandra Sue settled into her favorite cushy chair. She stretched her long lanky legs onto the flowered-chintz ottoman. As "101 Strings" strummed, she picked up her dog-eared copy of *When He Leaves*. The pages fell open in the flickering firelight, and she read, "There is a time for everything."

"You've got that right," Sandra Sue laughed. "Tomorrow it's time to go shopping!"

> *If you've gotten to this chapter, you know the joke's on him!*
>
> —KARI WEST

Lightening Up the Easy Way

Your luster is lasting. So is your smile. But it's more than a sunny disposition. There is light behind your eyes and passion in your voice. You're laughing again.

You are not a dry-clean-only item: stiff. Starched. Confined inside a stuffy bag. You're one swanky number who is comfortable with yourself. You've been through life's hot water and come out knowing what's true about yourself. You're not embarrassed by a little wear and tear or by wrinkles. You are no longer hanging out in the back of the closet.

What matters now isn't the way you looked to him or what he took from you, but the adventure of every tomorrow. "He turned my sorrow into joy!" wrote the psalmist. "He took away my clothes of mourning and clothed me with joy."[1] It's time to go shopping with God.

Today's women don't have hot flashes. They have power surges.

—NEW SAYING

Get the Last Laugh

"Happy hormones" like immunoglobulin and cytokines, experts say, fight bacteria and viruses and destroy tumors. Just a quarter hour of belly-laughing is enough aerobic activity to stimulate and increase the level of these hormones. Laughter stimulates blood circulation and oxygenation, which promotes clear thinking. It increases "natural killer" white blood cells, according to researchers Lee Berk and Arthur Stone.[2] Their studies suggest healing is accelerated in people who laugh.

We're Having a Pity Party—You're Invited!

Feeling the weight of the world on your shoulders? Don't be so glum, chum! Come to a pithy pity party for the dumped, downsized, exploited, allergic, neglected, ignored, bored, and doormats. It's the perfect escape for those who have drops that spot, no life, bad-hair days, the heartbreak of psoriasis, rebellious children, cranky creditors, and pets that aren't housebroken.

Dress is casual, but wear sackcloth and ashes if you prefer.

Comfort-food snacks, beer to cry in, and a new deck of cards (so you can change the hand life's dealt you) will be provided.

Please join us for this chance to laugh at life and ourselves.

—Michele (I-see-my-dog-more-than-
I-see-my-husband) Tennesen

"Put on a happy face" and "Fake it till you make it" are good advice. Other research shows that the act of smiling, even when you don't feel like it, can reduce stress and improve your mood.

Not only does it elicit positive responses from others, but it promotes a sense of well-being. According to psychologist Paul Ekman of the Human Interaction Lab at the University of California in San Francisco, real smiles and fake smiles produce identical changes in brain activity, skin temperature, heart rate, and respiration.[3]

"You can't just sit around waiting for the inspiration to become happier to strike you," says Dr. David Myers, professor of psychology at Hope College in Holland, Michigan, citing an international study of 170,000 people. "But it can help you take steps in the right direction." Myers believes, after researching hundreds of scientific studies on happiness, that with practice attitudes can follow behavior.[4]

Nobody ever died of laughter.
—MAX BEERBOHM

Let Life's Absurdities Tickle You Pink

Do whatever it takes to release those happy brain chemicals. Start exercising that muscle attached to your funny bone. With practice, you'll get the hang of it. Begin by compiling a humor profile. What were your favorite pass-the-time moments as a child? What activities made you really happy? Was it slapping together mud pies in the sandbox? Playing "Skip to my Lou"? Fishing with your big brother? Flying kites? What did you beg your mom and dad to do over and over again? As you grew up, what Sunday funnies did you read, and which comedians made you crack up? These are keys to what makes you feel good now.

Comedy is tragedy—plus time.
—CAROL BURNETT

Make a laughter scrapbook. Fill it with cartoons, jokes, stories, funny greeting cards, kids' sayings, and overheard comments that make you laugh. Read the funnies faithfully. Ask people to save and send you things that are humorous. Keep a pencil and paper by the TV so you can record one-liners that get you giggling. Spend a half hour chuckling at the card store. Write anything funny in your notebook.

> *Few women admit their age. Few men act theirs.*
> —AUTHOR UNKNOWN

Build a play box. Collect small toys, gag gifts, and whimsical items that are fun, colorful, and cuddly. Take a chuckle break and delve into it. Pull out a bottle of bubbles and blow them around the office. Disguise your voice with a foreign accent and leave a mysterious message on a friend's answering machine. Call your sister and tell her the latest "knock-knock" joke. Ask your kids for crazy riddles and rhymes.

> *You can tell it's going to be a bad day when...*
> * *you put your bra on backward and it fits better.*
> * *you call suicide prevention and they put you on hold.*
> * *your blind date turns out to be your ex-husband.*
> —PASSED ON AT A PITY PARTY SPOOF

Cultivate wacky humor in your family. Sometimes you have to turn to outside sources and a context totally beyond your own environment. When you find something everybody laughs at, you know it's a treasure. If you're tuned in, you can even turn insults into hilarity. Twist slaps into compliments; you'll drive your enemies crazy.

> *Climb every mountain. Ford every stream. Follow every rainbow. (That oughta reduce middle-age spread.)*
> —AUTHOR UNKNOWN

Ask: What will be important 100 years from now? That you got mad at your teenager's latest insult and tried to set him straight, or that you turned it into an occasion to laugh? You might also lift his heavy burdens, not by trying to "talk" about it, but by leaving things in his room that make him laugh. Tape clever sayings inside closets or tuck them under pillows. Leave a dollar—or five—where someone will find it—in the pocket of favorite jeans, the toe of a shoe, or a textbook. Catch him laughing with friends, and take notes on what works. Spread those feel-good hormones however and wherever you can.

> *Laughter is a tranquilizer with no side effects.*
> —ARNOLD GLASOW

Go Ahead and Lose it

It's never too late to loosen up. You are never too old. Celebrate what you thought was impossible by grinning at reality. A 100-year-old woman believed she was way beyond menopause and forever barren. In the end, God handed her a late, great bundle of joy. She laughed and said, "All who hear will laugh with me."[5]

Even your grandmother used to say, "Laugh and the world laughs with you. Cry and you cry alone."[6] How true that is! Rare friends will be there for you when you express vulnerabilities and need to let the tears flow. But most people don't have broad enough shoulders. They are personally threatened by your loss and don't know what to say about your grief. If you don't pick yourself up, eventually you will lose friends; it's just a fact of life.

Happiness attracts like a magnet. You will get others laughing with you. Laughter sweeps cobwebs out of closet corners and keeps the moths out. Starve the negative, and feed the positive. Make a list of all the good things about being single.

You no longer have to...

- explain buying another pair of shoes to go with the 16 you already have
- listen to snoring in the middle of the night
- share closet space
- filter things through his schedule
- ask his opinion
- shoo the cat off his car
- wrestle for the remote control
- make notes to remind him of everything
- be late because he won't ask directions
- worry about an unbalanced checkbook

On the weekends he gets the kids, you get to...

- sit in the big comfortable chair anytime at all
- turn up the heat as high as you like
- devour every chocolate-filled truffle in the box
- pick out the piece of chicken you really want
- leave dishes in the sink for two days

- order Betty Boop checks
- eat garlic bread
- create order (finally) in the garage

> *Laughter is a shock absorber that eases the blows of life.*
> —AUTHOR UNKNOWN

Only Your Hairdresser Knows for Sure

Noelle: Sue, my hairdresser, and I sat in her car outside the post office in pouring rain. I'll never forget how embarrassed and humiliated I felt. But I needed her advice on talking to my daughter Christy about Dan's imminent departure. Her son was Christy's longtime boyfriend, and I thought maybe he could help.

"I have something to tell you," I started. She could see I was in pain and interrupted by blurting, "Christy is pregnant!" Her comment, by its shock value, took me by surprise. I burst out laughing.

"No," I said. "Dan is having an affair."

Sue begged me to tell her who the other woman was. I refused.

"Okay," she said. "I'm going to say one name and if that isn't who it is, I'll shut up."

To my amazement, she knew!

"Look," Sue said, "I've been in the beauty shop for 17 years."

I couldn't help but chuckle. As if it were no big thing, Sue helped me see everything differently. "Tell Dan to move in with her," she advised. "I guarantee he'll be out in 14 days."

With a wise, earthy detachment, Sue exposed humor inherent in my pain. I craved her wit, her ability to make me feel better—unlike the comments of my superspiritual friends, who sometimes made me feel worse with their patronizing advice. That day what I needed most was a good-hearted poke in the ribs.

When Dan eventually approached Sue with his version of our saga, she wasn't fooled. She simply told him, "Noelle did what she had to do to cope with what you put her through."

To all the beauty-shop people everywhere who help us through those bad-hair days, I say, "Thank you for being real. Hurrah for hairdressers!"

Angels can fly because they take themselves lightly.
—C.K. CHESTERTON

Kari: Behind every dumped wife is a hairdresser story. For 30 years I've followed my hairdresser, Karen, from shop to shop through life's tragedies to its triumphs. She knew about Ed's affairs before I did. She cut The Neighbor's hair!

"Knowing that I knew and you didn't know, and not being able to say that I knew, was awful," she says now. Like a rock dropped into a pond, the rippling effect of the affair tested our friendship.

Determined that Ed's actions would not destroy it, I returned each month for a trim. Karen showed me The Neighbor wasn't a vixen but one of many victims. Karen is great at what she does. Who else but a hairdresser could have helped me wash that man out of my hair? By getting to the root of the problem and adding a little color to it, I saw that when Ed got kinky, the "perm" fell out of our marriage.

For quite a while Karen and I giggled like school girls about all the players in this comedy of errors: Ed, still acting out the same ol' role; The Neighbor and I, who took our bow years ago and moved on.

Reality is for people who lack imagination!
—BUMPER STICKER

Live on the Wild Side: Go for the Wacky

Hang out with hyenas: Go looking for things that make you crack up and double over. Curl up the corners of your mouth when you meet another person on the street. Keep a joke ready on your lips. Get as wacky as you need to be. Martin Luther said, "If you aren't allowed to laugh in heaven, I don't want to go there." More than a temporary "ha," grins and guffaws imprint joy in your brain and nervous system.

Wasn't it Albert Einstein who said, "Imagination is everything"? Then, why be normal? Open up your soul. You've made it this far. Don't get run down; wind up your wit. Get electric by plugging into humor.

> *Put on the new [wo]man.*
> —EPHESIANS 4:24

Noelle: "Queen of Dorkdom." That's what my youngest daughter calls me!

"And proud of it!" I reply.

One man I dated often told me, "You're nutty!" It was the greatest compliment. Had I ever before dared to be nutty, a dork, anything other than perfectly sensible?

After a visit with Christy at college one weekend, I asked her to walk me to my car to say goodbye. On the way to the dorm elevator we got to giggling about the rude sound my shoes made on the carpet. Suddenly, the elevator doors parted and 16 people stood staring straight-faced at Christy and me. We regained decorum, got on, and then promptly lost it, giggling all the way down to the ground floor.

> *Learn to laugh at your troubles and you'll never run out*
> *of things to laugh at.*
>
> —Lyn Karol

Kari: "Wipe that smile off your face," my parents often told my brother and me. "Don't laugh at the table or you'll be crying afterward." I took their advice the way they meant it: seriously. My great-grandparents homesteaded the prairie in dugouts, and their stern Midwestern life-is-tough mentality was passed down to me. I inherited more somber bones than silly ones.

My adult world was solemn, too; there were few laughs where I worked. So when Ed decided our marriage vows were a joke, I decided to make some changes of my own. I learned to "chill," as my daughter puts it. When she left for high school wearing a pair of those ready-to-drop baggy pants, I either had to laugh at myself or check into a psycho ward. Now you should see us having fun in the dressing rooms at Marshalls or Ross; these days Melanie is the one in a tiz over my shopping coups. She won't let me out of the fitting room in low-rider jeans.

Shopping with Noelle, I talked her into buying the three-inch heels (instead of the two-inch) and a silk shirt that flaps open softly at the neckline. We laughed all afternoon, exchanging parts of our stories we'd never dared tell. The first time I had assured her, "Someday you'll laugh," she was incredulous. Our chuckles now are not a spiteful "ha, ha, ha," but an exhalation and exclamation: "Aha! Now I get it!"

> *The most wasted of all our days are those in which we*
> *have not laughed.*
>
> —Nicolas-Sebastien Chamfort

She Smiles at the Future

In the beginning, life was simple. All you wanted was love. A little happiness. Health. A decent haircut. Into your mental scrapbook you pasted snapshots of the man and the marriage that was to last a lifetime. Somewhere along the way, he decided it was not to be.

Now, if you are courageous enough to feel, wise enough to forgive, strong enough to let go, and brave enough to have a vision, you, too, will laugh again. When he leaves, you decide what will be. Go ahead. Let 'er rip. You know the joke's on him!

I'm Laughing Again!

Here's what I laughed about this week…

This is how I know the joke's on him…

Heart Work

Chapter Sixteen

I Am Safe, Secure, and Loved

My people can safely camp in the wildest places...I will make my people and their homes around my hill a blessing...No one shall make them afraid.

—EZEKIEL 34:25,26,28 TLB

Kari: Birds' nests decorate the branches of a tree in my living room. I've been picking them up around my country garden for years. An oriole's palm-threaded hammock. The adobe flat of a swallow. A redwing blackbird's grass hut. A hummingbird suite. The twig-cabin of a scrub jay. And an anonymous shelter created from vacuum fuzz, dog hair, and scraps of twine.

My favorite nest is fashioned from the needles of a Christmas tree we tossed over the hillside a few years back. All summer the sun sizzled. Then winter winds blew. From the sharp, brittle needles of this abandoned noble fir, a bird wove a nest that spring. I discovered the masterpiece during fall cleanup. I'm fascinated how the dark needles are laced together with those sunbleached a dusty gray.

As I clean today, I remove the intricate little nest from its place and cradle it in my palm. At the top is a small opening. Prickly needles were curved around to protect the brood once nestled inside the tightly woven basket.

The nest affirms and inspires me. I know something about this: how the prickly protects. Finding something useful in discarded stuff that had lost meaning for someone else. Weaving past with present to cradle the future, the care and feeding of fledglings: my daughter and my incubating dreams. Not long ago I felt like that tossed-out Christmas tree. Discarded in midlife. Over the hill. Left alone to make it or break it.

One season followed the next. So much more has come. My life was created, not by accident but by design. I am discovering beauty in change. Making peace with contrast. Accepting uncertainty. Learning to like it here.

> *A man who strays from home is like a bird that wanders from its nest.*
> —PROVERBS 27:8 TLB

Spring: Time of Incubation

No matter what season the calendar shows, in your life it is spring—time for a new beginning. This season you and God are forming a weather-tight fortress made from whatever is available and profitable. This crash pad will house and protect your brood, your spirit, and your soul from predators and the elements until you are ready to fly. You are nesting, resting within the rustic comfort of this place. Some memories still prick when you go in and out and about your work. But you are safe here and secure. And never forget—you are loved.

He keeps his eye upon you as you come and go.
—PSALM 121:8 TLB

You Are Safe

You are safe because now you are responsible for yourself. You are no longer living under the influence of an unloving mate. Why he left isn't as important now as living in a way that is consistent with your character and what you know is true. You are safe because you have kept your dignity, your reputation, and your spirit. Through it all, you have not allowed evil to destroy your soul or take away your desire to live.

To you, home furnishes more than a covering called a house. It feeds inner peace and fosters calmer thoughts. When you pass through the opening of your own nesting place and close the door, you are safe to chat on the phone with your best friend, tuck your children into bed, and to read-till-you-drop words that bring sweet sleep. You may feel lonely when you lie there, but you are not alone. You are praying for angels to guard the four corners of your rooftop. You are putting weariness to rest under the shadow of God's wings.

You are safe when you rely on the people who love you and on the power of God. You no longer apologize for the intelligence or personality with which you are endowed, nor the discernment and resilience you've shown. You are protected by the boundaries you have clearly drawn between yourself and toxic people. You are safe because the past cannot control you. Without anger and rage attaching you to him, the power of the past is broken. His unhappiness is his problem; you cannot fix life for him. Your bold commitment to move forward with your life and not fall back into old patterns is a barrier he cannot penetrate.

You are breaking free of thoughts that harm your health and the worry that cuts off faith, strangles peace, and kills joy. You have stopped being your own worst enemy. Because you deserve God's best, you won't settle for less than that. You are covering blank walls with pictures of where you'd like to be. Portraits of hope. For the rest of your life, you will look for pivotal moments sandwiched between ordinary days.

> *Some people are always grumbling because roses have thorns. I am thankful that thorns have roses.*
> —ALPHONSE KARR

Noelle: A friend came over the other day to ask one of my daughters to babysit. We got to talking about other things, and she confided that, although her husband reconciled with her after his affair, she still feels a hole in her heart. "My love for him is not innocent and sweet the way it used to be," she said.

Sadness filled me. Seeing them back together, playing with their kids or working in their yard while I tackled mine alone, I'd felt a little envious, thinking, *That's the way it's supposed to happen.* Hearing her confession pulls me back to reality. No longer does my friend feel 100-percent safe in her husband's presence. I wanted to run over and shake that man. "Love her, you fool," I wanted to say. "Court her; give her yourself. Don't you understand what your mistake cost her? And don't you have any idea what you're missing?"

Now I know things will never be the same for either her or me. I don't know which is harder: being divorced and starting all over; or, like her, trying to put the pieces back together in the same, yet different, relationship. We have both been through something profound. I have decided to let it add something to my life rather than take away. It has given me an authenticity, an authority that wasn't there before, and a sense of presence with myself.

Am I being realistic? I don't know. But that's the beauty of redesign. You get another chance to tweak and flex as you go along. Nothing has to be perfect the first time—or ever. The more unexpected twists there are, the more creative you become in weaving them all together. I work hard at this, and I guess it shows. Yesterday I ran into the counselor who helped me through my earliest trauma. "You look good," she kept saying with admiration in her voice—as if she couldn't quite believe it.

> *One can never consent to creep when one feels an impulse to soar.*
>
> —HELEN KELLER

You Are Secure

You are secure because you have created sanctuary from recycled bits and pieces of your life. You have built it all in the shelter of sturdy, steady branches that bend with the wind. You are no longer vulnerable to the pseudo-provision of another person who did not have your best interests at heart.

The psalmist writes about security that comes from hands and fingers trained for daily battles and all-out war. God stands between you and your concerns and subdues them under you. Because of this, you seize each day even when you are trembling. You know that you can reinvent your life and redesign your nest as you see fit, as the Lord leads, as weather permits. Your spiritual guidelines have been tested and tried.

Your security is not tangible, like a retirement account, a family inheritance, or life-insurance policies. Your security comes from the inside out, from new emotional rules that push you toward your calling. You refuse to spend another day with the guilt that you could have done more. You know that no one can heal another's wounds. And you don't tolerate abuse anymore, just as you don't do gravy. You are learning when to move out of your own way.

No longer are you tied to other people's opinions or shaken by their criticism. Their definitions don't hold you back or pen you in. You are making distinctions that will pull you like a magnet toward God's will. You are incubating dreams. Believe it or not, you're in the right spot at the right time. You are here for a reason. Determine to live it out.

> *Merely sustaining life is a vegetative state…Thoroughly living life requires initiative, risk-taking, sustained action against odds, sacrificing for ideals and for others, leaps of faith. People who lead such lives report being happy, hopeful and exhilarated even when they fail.*
> —DR. LAURA SCHLESSINGER

Kari: Five years ago, with dreams of apple pie, I carved a hole in the hard clay. I pounded in a stake and tied a tree in a five-gallon bucket to it with a strip of insulated wire. Over time, the trunk grew over and around the restraining wire. Today all that's visible is an inch-wide scar ringing the trunk. I can't push the wire in or pull it out, but the tree has learned to live with it.

I am growing around and over life's "if onlys" just the way my tree did. Etched in my mind is not only the painful experience of divorce but God's faithfulness. I learned how important it is to press on with hope even when circumstances and changes would hold me back. To live with my scar, I've had to accept it as one of life's contrasts. Divorce is one piece in the collection of fragments that make up the whole of my life.

I understand when a friend says, "I can't do this anymore." I hear myself saying the same words in an office conference room years ago. After downing three cups of stale coffee, I wondered if I could hold back tears long enough to do my job that afternoon. But I did.

Somehow, one season at a time, I grew over and around my hampering wire. There's a certain security in the ongoing process of living. I can't live a year in a moment. I can't plant a fruit tree today and eat pie tomorrow. Each day I hope my life paints a word picture of what Anne Frank wrote: "I don't think of all the misery, but of all the beauty that still remains."[1]

> *We know that all things work together for good to those who love God, to those who are called according to His purpose.*
>
> —ROMANS 8:28

You Are Loved

You are loved whenever you enhance the life of someone else. You are loved when you choose to embrace your own life. When you act in loving ways toward yourself, you affirm what your heavenly Father says about you.

You are loved when you decide to accept and try to understand others regardless of who they are or how they treat you. You are loved when you welcome into your life the relentless Lover,

Almighty God. You are loved when you nurture intimacy with your family, passion for daily adventure, and devotion to the kingdom of heaven.

When you surround yourself with grand books, great music, and good people, you are loved. You are loved when you take care of both body and soul. You are loved when you reach out to touch the world: children, babies, the elderly, animals, the velvet petals of a blossom, and raindrops. Love comes when you hug others and allow them to come close enough to hug you. When you laugh or surprise yourself. When you follow your convictions, do what you know is right, live with a clear conscience. When you follow the way of the pure-hearted. When you hold tightly to the truth.

You are God's dearly beloved and the object of his affection. Chosen. The apple of his eye. Heir to his kingdom. He planned the redemption he makes real in you every day. When you respond by living your life with meaning, you reveal your commitment to the covenant between you and him. You owe it to yourself and to God to remember all the experiences of life, even if you feel they were unhappy. Living is about reconciling yourself to contrasts, like sweet and sour, as well as every nuance in between. Accepting that you are loved by God in spite of crises is a life-changing decision.

Love is a celebration of thanksgiving for receiving all you need to live fully. You fall out of love when you get hung up on what you want—the perfect husband, perfect marriage, perfect kids. A charmed life. You fall out of love when what you think you deserve gets in the way of gratitude for what you already have and always had.

You are loved because you take responsibility for your shortcomings, changing what you can and letting the Lord work on the rest.[2] You are loved because you belong in this world. To bless and not curse—or cure. To worship by using your gifts and talents to cultivate beauty and replenish hope. To care enough to make a difference. To love. In heaven's eyes, you are not half of something broken...you have been made whole.

> *To laugh often and much...that is to have succeeded.*
> —RALPH WALDO EMERSON

Noelle: Ten years have passed since the beginning of this story. My nest is empty now. My eldest child, married and a professional who makes doing career, family, and home look easy, is now incubating baby number two. (Yes, she did marry Todd!) My middle child, whose hard work won her scholarships and a job in the Big Apple, flits home at intervals and is planning a trip around the world. I hear the wings of my soulful college daughter, my youngest, flutter in rhythm. A poet and philosopher, her sensibilities for the less fortunate have caused her to reach for possibilities—with an international scope.

On the brink of changing directions myself, I listen as my firstborn reminds me, "Don't think of your age, Mom; it's as if you're just starting out. Your whole life lies ahead of you." Yes, I'm sandwiched now between caring for elderly parents and owning my dreams. But I'm not in Kansas anymore. I discover I'm savvy, sensual, and spiritual (and—well, a little sassy, too) on the yellow brick road of midlife. Instead of waiting around for somebody to rock my world, I'm clad in ruby slippers and in haute pursuit of new purpose. You might say I'm heading over the rainbow, not the hill.

> *Love makes you present in your own life.*
> —WHITNEY OTTO

A Time for Flight

The most beautiful and useful things in your life are those characterized by simplicity. You are off the hillside and in the process of redesign. The real love affair begins now. God is working with you. You are working with yourself.

You are coming to terms with your aloneness. It has nothing to do with whether you are in a new relationship or remarried. Being a couple is not validation for who you are. You are your own best companion. You are whole. When you are lonely, you accept that emotion as a universal cry of humanity. You are created for God and community. When you hurt, you migrate to people who know what to say to help you heal. You call them up. You seek them out. You see that their wise counsel cost them dearly. Like you, their lives are woven through with the contrasts of adversity and resilience. They offer credible comfort.

You count on others to be there. But even if they are not, you begin to believe in yourself. And you believe the Almighty God loves you through each changing season. You can bet your life on the fact that he is a lover who will never leave.

Faith goes up the stairs that love has made and looks out the window which hope has opened.
—C.H. SPURGEON

I Am Safe, Secure, and Loved

I will feather my nest with comforts. I want it to feel good to be home, so today I will do at least one thing to create ambience in

- my bedroom...
- the kitchen...
- the living room...

I will be good to myself and feed my soul. Here are three things I will do to get closer to myself and closer to God:

1.

2.

3.

Epilogue

—◌◌—

As we write the last lines, update everything that's changed since we started, and wrap up the final manuscript, our lives are still unfolding…

Noelle: I finally had skylights installed in my cottage, those symbols of clarity I had to postpone when my ex left. The change they make in my north-facing living room is greater than I had imagined, like the changes in my life since becoming single again. Certainly those intense changes caused me to confront many losses. Yet I've found each loss to be a threshold in disguise.

When my last child left the nest, I felt lost and desolate. But about the same time, an adorable granddaughter showed up in my life with coos, giggles, and peachy skin. When a romantic relationship crashed, I decided to learn to snowboard, toe-edging my way toward thrills on the slopes instead. When 9/11 created an economic tailspin, a vacuum in freelance editorial work forced me to write books of my own. Once I realized I needed a break from the country life, I rented my house, stored furnishings, and prepared to move on—in a literal way this time. Sleeping for the last time in that empty house, my feelings were not of sadness. That puzzled me, because my future was unclear.

I've since learned that every time we close a door behind us— or even when someone else slams it shut against our will—we find ourselves standing on a new threshold. As this book is completed, my fiancé and I are laying our one-year engagement on the shelf. Though we are both still deeply in love, we are experiencing the reality that midlife remarriages are full of complicated issues and difficult decisions.

One thing I know for certain: The love and a man and the security of marriage are never cure-alls. They merely stand among many doorways and possibilities. What's clear is that regardless of what I choose, only faith and fortitude will empower me to live with purpose. God invites me to thrive regardless of my marital state. I've decided to participate with passion in the adventure, wherever the road may lead.

Kari: Not long ago, Melanie and I were driving to the mall, talking about finally becoming friends and reminiscing about all those years she hated me. "Mom, don't you get it?" she asked. "You were the rock; you never moved. I love my dad a lot, but I couldn't count on him. Sure, I could do anything I wanted at his house, but I never knew where he stood."

I remembered the many times I had retreated to the sanctuary of my bedroom, out of answers and out of strength. I had lifted my weary arms to the sky, imagining my daughter lying across my open palms, and prayed, "Lord, you've got a big problem. I don't know what to do anymore. I'm tired and scared. Melanie is yours; I give her back to you."

In those desperate moments, I was leaning on a strength greater than my own and on a love broader than I could imagine at the time. Only with hindsight can I see what was there all along and always will be: an unchangeable God, who treasures my tears and is my immovable rock. Jesus, who intercedes for me. The Holy Spirit, who leads me into truth and understands when the only language I have is my tears.

Enveloped in the days that follow are precious moments for embracing what comes and pivotal moments for letting go. With each changing season in my garden and in my life, I take heart, knowing that after today's sunset comes tomorrow's sunrise.

You Are Not Alone

You are not alone. With us, you are going through something profound. Perhaps you still cannot make sense of it. When godless powers work overtime, it is to divert your progress. They want you stuck in the shadows of your fear and their lies. A consequence of divorce is that the old luggage you thought you had stashed away keeps falling out and flopping open. From time to time you have to resort and repack the same stuff. Don't let that fact rattle you. This is simply the way it is.

Although you cannot once and for all vindicate the truth, you hold tightly to it. You know truth needs no defense. So when you can't go back, you go on. Each step you take forward moves you toward life and light. You will never know how many others will be helped along the way.

We whisper, "Keep moving; keep going."

Your snapshots are still being developed.

You can live and let live. Just because you lost the love of a man doesn't mean you won't have the last laugh!
—KARI AND NOELLE

The Power of Divorce Is an Illusion

It doesn't rip off your relationship with God.
It wilts under the heat of passion for life.
It stops short of robbing every hope.
It fades in the light of good humor.
It doesn't disrobe you of dignity.
It cannot take your courage.
It is dis-empowered by joy.
It capitulates to optimism.
It is disarmed by truth.
Its pain is temporary.
It is starved by faith.
Its time is limited.
(You'll see!)

Notes

Chapter 2—Kari's Snapshots

1. From the hymn, "I Would Be True," words by Howard A. Walter, 1906.

Chapter 3—Noelle's Snapshots

1. From the "Wedding Song" by Noel Paul Stookey, Public Domain Foundation, Inc., 1971.

2. Statistics from Family Safe Media, "Pornography Statistics 2003" ("derived from a number of different reputable sources including Google, WordTracker, PBS, MSNBC, NRC, and Alexa research"), www.familysafemedia.com/pornography_statistics.html, 7/27/2004.

3. Statistics collected by The National Coalition for the Protection of Children & Families (NCPCF Online), "Current Statistics," http://nationalcoalition.org/stat.html, 7/27/2004. Original sources are, respectively, Rebecca Hagelin, "Overdosing on Porn," www.world andi.com, March 2004; "The Architects of Porn," *VARBusiness*, 28 April 2000; "Pornography Statistics 2003," Family Safe Media, www.familysafemedia.com, 2003; "Internet Pornography Statistics 2003," David C. Bissette, Psy.D., www.healthymind .com, 2004; National Coalition survey of pastors, Seattle, April 2000; *Sex on TV: Content and Context,* The Kaiser Family Foundation, 5 February 2001, and "More TV Sex," *USA Today,* 30 March 2000; Linda Greenhouse, "Court Overrules Law Restricting Cable Sex Shows," *The New York Times On the Web*; "New look at TV sex and violence," *National Catholic Register* quoting The Center for Media and Public Affairs, 16-22 April 2000.

Chapter 4—I Have God and Me

1. Michael Haederle, "Divorcees Say, 'Take This!' To Their Rings," *Los Angeles Times*, date n/a.

2. Helen Richards, "God's Protection During War and Peace," broadcast interview Tape No. CS 332/2131 (Colorado Springs, CO: Focus on the Family).

3. "The Sad Truth About Christians and Marriage," *The Barna Report*, Premiere Issue, pp. 5-6. See also the Barna Group, *The Barna Update,* December 12, 2000, "The Year's Most Intriguing Findings," www.barna.org/FlexPage.aspx?Page=BarnaUpdate &BarnaUpdateID=77.

4. Karen Peterson, "A smattering of secrets from successful couples," *USA Today,* Feb. 27, 1996; excerpted from Neil Clark Warren, *The Triumphant Marriage: 100 Extremely Successful Couples Reveal Their Secrets* (Colorado Springs, CO: Focus on the Family, 1996).

5. Peter Kramer, "For Better or Worse," *Elle*, September 1997, pp. 306-308.

6. Michael Gartner, "Values? What about divorce?" *USA Today*, June 6, 1995, p. 13A; excerpted from 1995 edition of *Information Please Almanac*.

7. "What about Divorce Statistics?" www.marriage-relationships.com/divorce_statistics .html, 7/27/04.

8. "Divorces carry financial sting for many middle-age women," *The Daily Review*, April 29, 1993, p. A-1,16; excerpts from U.S. Census Bureau Data 8.

9. Gail Sheehy, *New Passages: Mapping Your Life Across Time* (New York: Ballantine, 1996).

10. "What about Divorce Statistics?"

11. "What about Divorce Statistics?"

12. "What about Divorce Statistics?"

13. Philip Yancey, *Where Is God When It Hurts?* (Grand Rapids, MI: Zondervan, 1990), p. 207.

14. Jim Smoke, *Growing Through Divorce* (Eugene, OR: Harvest House, 1995), p. 150.

15. Dwight Small, *Remarriage and God's Renewing Grace* (Grand Rapids, MI: Baker Book House, 1986), pp. 43,50,51.

16. "What Crisis?" *Life*, November 1995, p. 76.

Chapter 5—My Hope Is Increasing

1. C.S. Lewis, *Mere Christianity* (New York: Macmillan, 1952), pp. 173-174.

2. Philip Yancey, *Disappointment with God* (Grand Rapids, MI: Zondervan, 1988), p. 204.

3. Psalm 139:18.

Chapter 6—I Need Time to Feel So I Can Heal

1. Barbara Lang Stern, "Your Well Being," *Vogue,* date n/a.

2. Malachi 2:16.

3. Genesis 2:18.

4. Ephesians 5:23-32.

5. John Townsend, *Hiding From Love* (Colorado Springs, CO: NavPress, 1991), p. 62. Townsend's current practice is Cloud-Townsend Communications, 260 Newport Center Drive, Ste. 430, Newport Beach, CA 92660.

6. Brenda Hunter, *Beyond Divorce* (Old Tappan, NJ: Fleming Revell, 1978), pp. 36,141.

7. Launa Herrmann, "Beyond the Anger of Divorce," *The Plain Truth*, March/April 1997, p. 20.

8. Archibald Hart, *Growing Up Divorced* (Ann Arbor, MI: Servant Publications, 1991), pp. 105-106.

9. Philip Yancey, *Disappointment with God* (Grand Rapids, MI: Zondervan, 1988) p. 94.

10. Psalm 51:17.

11. Matthew 5:4.

12. Michael Ryan, "Go Ahead, Cry," *Parade*, Jan. 5, 1997.

13. Ryan.

14. Romans 8:26-27; John 11:35; Jeremiah 9:1; Revelation 21:4; Luke 7:38; Psalm 56:8.

15. Ecclesiastes 3:4-8 TLB.

16. M. Scott Peck, *The Road Less Traveled* (New York: Simon & Schuster, 1978), p. 278.

17. Matthew 11:28.

18. John Townsend, *Hiding From Love* (Colorado Springs, CO: NavPress, 1991), pp. 100-101.

19. Proverbs 13:12.

20. Proverbs 27:19.

21. Marlee Alex, "Family Values," *Aspire*, January 1997, pp. 19-20.

Chapter 7—I Am Giving Myself a Chance

1. Psalm 17:8; 91:2; 119:114; Song of Solomon 2:14; Proverbs 18:10.

2. Isaiah 45:15.

3. Isaiah 45:3.

4. Psalm 119:133.

5. Isaiah 26:3 KJV.

6. Ephesians 1:18-19 MSG.

7. 1 Corinthians 2:16.

8. Elinor Levy, PhD, and Tom Monte, "The Medicine Within," *Ladies' Home Journal*, April 1997, p. 58; and Catherine Houck, "When Stress Gets Under Your Skin," *Good Housekeeping*, May 1996, p. 52.

9. Proverbs 18:14.

10. Gerald Sittser, *A Grace Disguised* (Grand Rapids MI: Zondervan, 1996).

11. Jan Miller Girando, Mary Engelbreit, illus., *Don't Look Back* (Kansas City, MO: Andrews and McMeel, 1994), last page.

12. Isaiah 54:11-12,14.

13. Psalm 139:1.

Chapter 8—I Am Not Disappearing

1. Tom Carter, ed., *2200 Quotations from the Writings of Spurgeon* (Grand Rapids, MI: Baker Books, 1988), p. 123.

2. Job 6:3 TLB.

3. Job 19:10.

4. Job 19:25.

5. 1 Kings 19:1-8.

6. Genesis 16:6-13.

7. Jack Hayford, *A New Time and Place* (Sisters, OR: Multnomah, 1997), p. 1.

8. Hayford, p. 25.

9. Hayford, pp. 27,29.

10. Philippians 1:6.

11. 2 Corinthians 4:16.

12. Daniel 7:25.

13. Ecclesiastes 11:4-5.

14. Matthew 14:15-20.

15. Joshua 1:3.

16. Joni Eareckson Tada, "Seeing the Impossible," *Moody* magazine, Nov. 1993, p. 32.

17. 1 Chronicles 4:10.

18. Habakkuk 3:16-19.

19. Deuteronomy 1:36 NASB.

Chapter 9—It's Okay to Lighten Up and Let Go

1. Colossians 1:17.

2. Philippians 3:12-13 KJV.

3. James Hillman, *The Soul's Code* (New York: Random House, 1996), pp. 41,43.

4. Hebrews 12:1.

5. Matthew 6:10.

6. Proverbs 31:30.

7. Psalm 139:5,8-10.

8. Ron Lee Davis, *A Forgiving God in an Unforgiving World* (Eugene, OR: Harvest House, 1984) p. 44.

9. Deuteronomy 33:27.

10. C.S. Lewis, from a letter "To Mrs. L."

11. Ingrid Trobisch, *Keeper of the Springs* (Sisters, OR: Multnomah, 1997), p. 9.

12. Adapted from "Newseyes: Give up the family jewels," *The Daily Review*, September 28, 1995.

13. Adapted from Cathy Horyn, "Diana Reborn," *Vanity Fair*, July 1997, p. 71.

14. Joni Eareckson Tada, *Joni Appointment Calendar 1986* (World Wide Pictures, 1985), January entry.

Chapter 10—My Ticket Outta Here

1. Historical data provided by Judy Buckingham, wife of Crater Lake National Park Head Ranger, George Buckingham, in a 1997 interview with Kari West.

2. Archibald Hart, *Growing Up Divorced* (Ann Arbor, MI: Servant Publications, 1991), p. 105.

3. Malcolm Boyd, *Rich with Years* (San Francisco: HarperSanFrancisco, 1994), entry for Feb. 7.

4. Job 31:30 NASB.

5. John Splinter, *The Complete Divorce Recovery Handbook* (Grand Rapids, MI: Zondervan, 1992), p. 110.

6. Exodus 12:21-23.

Chapter 11—I Am Going to Make It

1. Sonya Friedman, "Isn't It Time to Please Yourself?" *Redbook*, February 1991, p. 154.

2. Deirdre Donahue, "A Tragic Peak," *USA Today*, April 24, 1997, pp. D1-D2.

3. Adapted from Anne Taylor Fleming, "The Other Side of the Mountain," *Ladies' Home Journal*, June 1997, p. 134.

4. Friedman, p. 154.

5. Dwight Small, *Remarriage and God's Renewing Grace* (Grand Rapids, MI: Baker Book House, 1986), p. 167.

6. Panel discussion with Laurie Hall, Noelle Quinn, and Kari West, "The Hidden Enemy of Marriage," Tape No. CT 009/1709 (Colorado Springs, CO: Focus on the Family).

7. "The Sad Truth About Christians and Marriage," *The Barna Report*, Premiere Issue, pp. 5-6. See also the Barna Group, *The Barna Update,* December 12, 2000, "The Year's Most Intriguing Findings," www.barna.org/FlexPage.aspx?Page=BarnaUpdate &BarnaUpdateID=77.

8. Ray DeVries, *Westmont College Alumni Newsletter*, February 1988, p. 3.

9. "The Ravages of Divorce," *The Barna Report*, vol. 1, no. 4:6.

10. Monica Gyulai, "Study finds divorce deeply scars kids," *The Daily Review*, June 3, 1997, pp. B-1-B-2.

11. Judith Wallerstein, Sandra Blakeslee, *Second Chances* (New York: Tichnor & Fields, 1989), p. 300.

12. "A Safe Place," *Virtue*, May/June 1994, p. 65.

13. "Your Letters," *Virtue*, January/February 1997; p. 8, referencing "'Tis the Season for Turmoil" by Kari West, *Virtue,* November/December 1996, pp. 37-40.

14. "Your Letters," *Virtue*, March/April 1997, p. 10 (referencing Kari West article).

15. Sam Keen, *The Passionate Life* (New York: HarperCollins, 1992) p. 248.

16. Jerry Bridges, *The Practice of Godliness* (Colorado Springs, CO: NavPress, 1983), p. 216.

Chapter 12—It's Time to Thrive

1. Dory Hollander, *101 Lies Men Tell Women and Why Women Believe Them* (New York: HarperCollins, 1995), p. 271.

2. "Medinews," *Ladies' Home Journal*, October 1995, p. 104; Nancy Wartik, "The surprising link to longer life," *McCalls*, June 1997, p. 108.

Chapter 13—I Like the New Me

1. Historical data provided by Alameda County, California, research librarians and "Winchester Mystery House," published for Winchester Mystery House, San Jose, California.

2. Luke 11:34-36.

3. Psalm 15:1 NASB.

4. John 14:6.

5. Proverbs 31:25 NIV.

6. Proverbs 1:20; 2:2-5 (both authors' paraphrase).

7. Isaiah 5:20; Proverbs 3:15; Job 28:18; Proverbs 1:1-6.

8. John Townsend, Henry Cloud, *Boundaries* (Grand Rapids, MI: Zondervan, 1992), p. 13.

9. Joshua 15:19.

10. Judges 4:8.

11. Judges 5:12,31.

12. Patricia Evans, *The Verbally Abusive Relationship* (Holbrook, MA: Bob Adams, Inc., 1992), p. 13.

13. Material provided in an interview of Jeff Klippenes by Kari West, Oct. 1997.

14. Genesis 3:7-8.

15. Genesis 3:2-6; 1 Corinthians 13:12 KJV.

16. 1 Corinthians 2:7-13.

17. Proverbs 3:5.

18. John 16:13.

19. Mark 6:51-52 NASB; Ecclesiastes 1:18 NASB.

20. Psalm 111:10.

21. Townsend, Cloud, p. 109.

22. Andrea Stone, "President's daughter makes up for lost time," *USA Today*, May 7, 1997, p. 4D.

23. Galatians 5:13.

24. Matthew 8:22.

25. Esther 4:16.

26. Jean Lush, "Enhancing the Larger Life," *Virtue*, Jan/Feb. 1993, p. 22.

27. Isabella Rossellini, *Some of Me* (New York: Random House, 1997), quoted in *Ladies' Home Journal*, September 1997.

28. John 10:7.

Chapter 14—My Children Are Listening

1. Statistics compiled by M. Franco Salvoza from National Fatherhood Initiative, as cited in "Father Figures," *USA Today Weekend*, June 14-16, 1996, p. 5; David Proenoe, "Life Without Father," *Reader's Digest*, Feb. 1997, p. 65, condensed from *Life Without Father* (New York: Simon & Schuster, Inc., 1996); "Single-Parent Families on the Rise," *Awake!* October 8, 2002, Watch Tower Bible and Tract Society of Pennsylvania, www.watchtower.org/legrary/g/2002/10/8/article_01.htm.

2. Judith Wallerstein, *Second Chances: Men, Women & Children a Decade After Divorce* (New York: Tichnor & Fields, 1989) pp. 301-302.

3. Judith Wallerstein, Joan B. Kelly, *Surviving the Breakup* (New York: Basic Books, Inc./Harper Torchbooks, 1980), p. 95; Judith S.Wallerstein, Julia M. Lewis, Sandra Blakeslee, *The Unexpected Legacy of Divorce* (New York: Hyperion, 2000), p. 308.

4. Wallerstein, Kelly, p. 95.

5. Isolina Ricci, *Mom's House, Dad's House* (New York: Macmillan, 1980) p. 180.

6. As quoted in "Tell Us What You Think," *Glamour*, June 1996.

7. "Tell Us What You Think."

8. Proverbs 23:10-11.

Chapter 15—I'm Laughing Again

1. Psalm 30:11-12 TLB.

2. "Laugh it off and live longer," *The Sunday Times*, Edinburgh, Scotland, August 11, 1996, pp. 1,20.

3. "Mind & Body: World's Cheapest Stressbuster—A Smile," *Good Housekeeping*, January 1995, p. 27.

4. John B. Thomas, "Health: How to Be Happier," *Better Homes and Gardens*, July 1993, pp. 66-67.

5. Genesis 21:6.

6. Ella Wheeler Wilcox, "Solitude."

Chapter 16—I Am Safe, Secure, and Loved

1. Anne Frank, *The Diary of Anne Frank* (New York: Simon & Schuster, 1952), p. 154.

2. Psalm 138:8.

Chapter-by-Chapter
Guide to Topics

Chapter 2—Kari's Snapshots
abuse, verbal and emotional
affairs, discovery
anger
   yours
   your child's
blame
celebration, when you see failure as a
   fresh start not a finish
child
   birth of
   hyperactive and learning-disabled
childhood dreams
deception
desertion
disbelief
divorce, arrival of summons
family holiday traditions
fear
God, wondering how he'll turn evil
   into good this time
marriage
   ceremony and vows
   downward spiral
midlife crisis, his
minister's advice
"Neighbor, The"
pornographic video
pornography
praying
   for child
   for a miracle
   for truth

suspicions
working late, his

Chapter 3—Noelle's Snapshots
abuse, verbal and emotional
affairs
   discovery
   suspicion
   his confession
blame
celebration, for life
childhood dreams
children, birth of
deception
fear
God, when you can't believe this is
   happening to you
love letters, discovery of
marriage
   ceremony and vows
   downward spiral
midlife crisis, his
"Neighbor, The"
pornographic video
pornography
praying, for the marriage
suspicions

Chapter 4—I Have God and Me
AIDS, your need for testing
cheating, patterns of
counseling, why he goes
divorce, statistics
divorce, worse than Dachau

More from Author Kari West

To subscribe to the e-mail version of the *DivorceWise Newsletter,* visit Kari's Web site:

www.GardenGlories.com

To receive the newsletter by regular mail, write to the following address:

Take Hope to Heart™
PO Box 11692
Pleasanton, CA 94588

If you would like to schedule Kari as a speaker for your event, visit the following Web site for further details and booking information:

www.TakeHopeToHeart.com

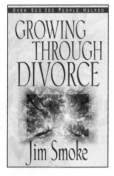

Growing Through Divorce

Jim Smoke

As you go through divorce, you are forced to accept drastic changes, make lifestyle-altering decisions, and develop new coping skills. In this bestselling resource, Jim Smoke draws on insights garnered through years of helping people survive divorce and offers you step-by-step guidance on such topics as...

- committing the situation to God through prayer
- helping children adjust
- seeking legal advice
- income issues
- contemplating remarriage

Discussion questions and a "working guide" section will help you take stock of your situation, handle day-to-day details, and eventually rediscover hope and joy in your life.

Successful Single Parenting

Gary Richmond

From years of experience with parents, Gary Richmond offers the most complete guide available for navigating the challenging waters of single parenting. You'll find advice on how to

- talk with your children about your love, the absence of the other parent, and more
- balance your needs with the needs of your children
- deal with financial changes
- work with the other parent for consistency in values and discipline
- handle visitation rights, child support, and remarriage issues

The Comforting Presence of God
Nancie Carmichael

In these warm and personal devotions, speaker and writer Nancie Carmichael shares her answers to the heart questions that come when you're experiencing the unavoidable changes life brings in family, work, and relationships:

- *What can I do when it seems nobody understands…when there's nobody I can talk to?*
- *I know I've messed up…how can I ever get right with God?*
- *I've done it all "right," and things are still falling apart. What now?*

Throughout the seasons of life, Nancie says, you can experience God as your mighty Rock, the One who never changes and who always comforts you.

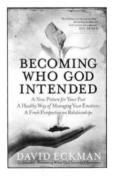

Becoming Who God Intended
David Eckman

Whether you realize it or not, your imagination is filled with *pictures* of reality. The Bible indicates these pictures reveal your true "heart beliefs"—the beliefs that actually shape your everyday feelings and reactions to family, friends, and others, to life's circumstances, and to God.

David Eckman compassionately shows you how to allow God's Spirit to build new, *biblical* pictures in your heart and imagination. As you do this, you will be able to accept God's acceptance of you in Christ, break free of negative emotions and habitual sin…and finally experience the life God the Father has always intended for you.

One-Minute Prayers™ for Those Who Hurt

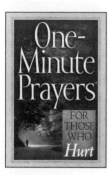

Harvest House Publishers

This collection of personal prayers and Scriptures leads you to rest during a hectic schedule, directs you to God's will during confusing times, and leads you to the Lord's mending touch when you're broken. You'll find encouragement to

- put words to your pain and lift yourself to God
- find solace and support in prayer
- understand that hope is the gift of today
- see trials as a path to victory
- reach beyond fear to embrace faith

Praying Through the Tough Times

By Lloyd John Ogilvie

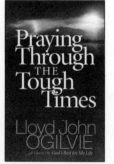

Perhaps you feel empty...disconnected...worn down by the difficulties of life and relationships. God seems distant. You find it difficult to pray.

Longtime pastor and bestselling author Lloyd John Ogilvie understands the tough times from his own experience. In this book of 100 prayers he offers ways to ask the Lord to clear your vision so you can...

- see the tough situations in light of His solutions
- see the difficult people you love through His eyes
- see an uncertain future transformed when you place it in His hands

As these prayers help you reconnect with the God who cares about you and wants to comfort you, He will guide you from panic to His perspective...and then to peace.

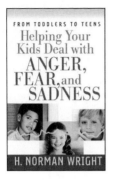

Helping Your Kids Deal with Anger, Fear, and Sadness

by H. Norman Wright

No parent wants to see their child struggle, especially with dark emotions such as anger, fear, and sadness. It's difficult to admit your child might be oppressed by these feelings, but this book can help. Family counselor and bestselling author Norm Wright addresses these emotional issues in a compassionate, family-friendly way that will enable you as a parent to bring comfort and a fresh perspective to your children.

Included in this interactive manual are conversational guidelines and learning activities for children that will encourage them to work through their difficult emotions. You as a parent will gain keen insights into the cause of these intense moods and be able to develop sound principles in dealing effectively with them.

Biblically-based and solution-oriented, *Helping Your Kids Deal with Anger, Fear, and Sadness* is an invaluable tool for parents who want to help their children and love and understand them better.